THE YALE SHAKESPEARE

Revised Edition

General Editors

Helge Kökeritz and Charles T. Prouty

THE YALE SHAKESPEARE

THE LIFE OF
HENRY THE FIFTH

Edited by R. J. Dorius

NEW HAVEN : YALE UNIVERSITY PRESS

FIRST PUBLISHED, SEPTEMBER, 1918
REVISED EDITION, OCTOBER, 1955
SECOND PRINTING, SEPTEMBER, 1959
THIRD PRINTING, MARCH, 1961

Published on the fund
given to the Yale University Press in 1917
by the members of the
Kingsley Trust Association
(Scroll and Key Society of Yale College)
to commemorate the seventy-fifth anniversary
of the founding of the society

Preface of the General Editors

AS the late Professor Tucker Brooke has observed, practically all modern editions of Shakespeare are 18th-century versions of the plays, based on the additions, alterations, and emendations of editors of that period. It has been our purpose, as it was Professor Brooke's, to give the modern reader Shakespeare's plays in the approximate form of their original appearance.

About half the plays appeared in quarto form before the publication of the First Folio in 1623. Thus for a large number of plays the only available text is that of the Folio. In the case of quarto plays our policy has been to use that text as the basis of the edition, unless it is clear that the text has been contaminated.

Interesting for us today is the fact that there are no act or scene divisions in the Quartos with the exception of *Othello*, which does mark Acts I, II, IV, and V but lacks indications of scenes. Even in the Folio, although act divisions are generally noted, only a part of the scenes are divided. In no case, either in Quarto or Folio, is there any indication of the place of action. The manifold scene divisions for the battle in such a play as *Antony and Cleopatra*, together with such locations as "Another part of the field," are the additions of the 18th century.

We have eliminated all indications of the place and time of action, because there is no authority for them in the originals and because Shakespeare gives such information, when it is requisite for understanding the play, through the dialogue of the actors. We have been sparing in our use of added scene and, in some cases, act divisions, because these frequently impede the flow of the action, which in Shakespeare's time was curiously like that of modern films.

Spelling has been modernized except when the original clearly indicates a pronunciation unlike our own, e.g. *desart* (desert), *divel* (devil), *banket* (banquet), and often in such Elizabethan syncopations as *ere* (e'er), *stolne* (stol'n), and *tane* (ta'en). In reproducing such forms we have followed the inconsistent usage of the original.

We have also preserved the original capitalization when this is a part of the meaning. In like manner we have tended to adopt the lineation of the original in many cases where modern editors print prose as verse or verse as prose. We have, moreover, followed the original punctuation wherever it was practicable.

In verse we print a final *-ed* to indicate its full syllabic value, otherwise *'d*. In prose we have followed the inconsistencies of the original in this respect.

Our general practice has been to include in footnotes all information a reader needs for immediate understanding of the given page. In somewhat empiric fashion we repeat glosses as we think the reader needs to be reminded of the meaning. Further information is given in notes (indicated by the letter *N* in the footnotes) to be found at the back of each volume. Appendices deal with the text and sources of the play.

Square brackets indicate material not found in the original text. Long emendations or lines taken from another authoritative text of a play are indicated in the footnotes for the information of the reader. We have silently corrected obvious typographical errors.

CONTENTS

[THE ACTORS' NAMES

KING HENRY THE FIFTH
DUKE OF GLOUCESTER ⎤
DUKE OF BEDFORD ⎬ *brothers to the king*
DUKE OF CLARENCE ⎦
DUKE OF EXETER, *uncle to the king*
DUKE OF YORK, *cousin to the king*
EARL OF SALISBURY
EARL OF WESTMORELAND
EARL OF WARWICK
ARCHBISHOP OF CANTERBURY
BISHOP OF ELY
EARL OF CAMBRIDGE
LORD SCROOP
SIR THOMAS GREY
SIR THOMAS ERPINGHAM ⎤
GOWER, *an English captain* ⎥ *officers in King Henry's*
FLUELLEN, *a Welsh captain* ⎬ *army*
MACMORRIS, *an Irish captain* ⎥
JAMY, *a Scottish captain* ⎦
JOHN BATES ⎤
ALEXANDER COURT ⎬ *soldiers in the same*
MICHAEL WILLIAMS ⎦
PISTOL
NYM
BARDOLPH
BOY
A HERALD
CHORUS

CHARLES THE SIXTH, *King of France*
LEWIS, *the Dauphin*
DUKE OF BURGUNDY
DUKE OF ORLEANS

ix

THE ACTORS' NAMES

DUKE OF BERRI
DUKE OF BRITAINE
DUKE OF BOURBON
THE CONSTABLE OF FRANCE
RAMBURES ⎫
GRANDPRÉ ⎬ *French lords*
BEAUMONT ⎭
GOVERNOR OF HARFLEUR
MONTJOY, *a French herald*
AMBASSADORS TO THE KING OF ENGLAND

ISABEL, *Queen of France*
KATHARINE, *daughter to Charles and Isabel*
ALICE, *a lady attending on her*
Hostess of the Boar's Head tavern in Eastcheap (formerly Mistress Quickly, now married to Pistol)

Lords, Ladies, Officers, French and English Soldiers, Citizens, Messengers, and Attendants

Scene: England and France]

The Actors' Names N. (N refers throughout to the corresponding note given at the end of the text.)

x

Enter Prologue.

O for a Muse of fire, that would ascend
The brightest heaven of invention,
A kingdom for a stage, princes to act,
And monarchs to behold the swelling scene!
Then should the warlike Harry, like himself,   5
Assume the port of Mars, and at his heels,
Leash'd in like hounds, should famine, sword, and fire
Crouch for employment. But pardon, gentles all,
The flat unraised spirits that hath dar'd
On this unworthy scaffold to bring forth   10
So great an object. Can this cockpit hold
The vasty fields of France? Or may we cram
Within this wooden O the very casques
That did affright the air at Agincourt?
O, pardon! since a crooked figure may   15
Attest in little place a million,
And let us, ciphers to this great accompt,
On your imaginary forces work.
Suppose within the girdle of these walls
Are now confin'd two mighty monarchies,   20

SD Prologue. SD is used throughout to refer to stage direction N. 2 invention poetic creation; -ion is frequently dissyllabic, as in l. 16. 6 port bearing. 8 gentles gentle audience. 9 unraised uninspired. spirits . . . hath N. 10 scaffold stage. 11 cockpit N. 12 vasty vast. 13 wooden O wooden circle N. casques helmets. 15 crooked figure N. 16 Attest stand for. 17 accompt means and is pronounced 'account.' 18 imaginary forces powers of imagination

Whose high upreared and abutting fronts
The perilous narrow ocean parts asunder.
Piece out our imperfections with your thoughts.
Into a thousand parts divide one man,
And make imaginary puissance. 25
Think when we talk of horses that you see them
Printing their proud hoofs i' th' receiving earth.
For 'tis your thoughts that now must deck our kings,
Carry them here and there, jumping o'er times,
Turning th' accomplishment of many years 30
Into an hourglass. For the which supply,
Admit me Chorus to this history,
Who prologue-like your humble patience pray
Gently to hear, kindly to judge, our play. *Exit.*

21 **abutting fronts** i.e. coasts of Dover and Calais. 22 **perilous** dissyllabic, and often written 'parlous.' 23 **Piece out** supplement. 25 **puissance** forces, troops (here a trisyllable). 27 **proud** spirited. 28 **deck** equip. 29 **jumping o'er times** the historical period of the play is 1414–20. 31 **supply** service.

Act I

SCENE 1

*Enter the two Bishops—[the Archbishop] of
Canterbury and [the Bishop of] Ely.*

Canterbury. My lord, I'll tell you. That self bill is
urg'd
Which in th' eleventh year of the last king's reign
Was like, and had indeed against us pass'd,
But that the scambling and unquiet time
Did push it out of farther question.   5
  Ely. But how, my lord, shall we resist it now?
  Canterbury. It must be thought on. If it pass
against us,
We lose the better half of our possession.
For all the temporal lands which men devout
By testament have given to the Church   10
Would they strip from us—being valu'd thus:
As much as would maintain to the king's honor
Full fifteen earls and fifteen hundred knights,
Six thousand and two hundred good esquires;
And, to relief of lazars and weak age,   15
Of indigent faint souls past corporal toil,
A hundred almshouses right well supplied;
And to the coffers of the king beside,

1 **self** same. 2 **eleventh year** 1410. 3 **like** likely (to pass). 4 **scambling** turbulent. 5 **question** consideration. 7–19 **It must . . . the bill** N. 9 **temporal** i.e. not used for religious purposes. 15 **lazars** diseased beggars, especially lepers. 16 **corporal** read 'corp'ral' N. 17 **supplied** N.

A thousand pounds by th' year. Thus runs the bill.
Ely. This would drink deep.
Canterbury.   'Twould drink the cup and all.
Ely. But what prevention?   21
Canterbury. The king is full of grace and fair re-
    gard.
Ely. And a true lover of the holy Church.
Canterbury. The courses of his youth promis'd it
    not.
The breath no sooner left his father's body,   25
But that his wildness, mortified in him,
Seem'd to die too. Yea, at that very moment,
Consideration like an angel came
And whipp'd th' offending Adam out of him,
Leaving his body as a paradise   30
T' envelop and contain celestial spirits.
Never was such a sudden scholar made;
Never came reformation in a flood
With such a heady currance, scouring faults,
Nor never Hydra-headed willfulness   35
So soon did lose his seat, and all at once,
As in this king.
   Ely.   We are blessed in the change.
  Canterbury. Hear him but reason in divinity,
And, all-admiring, with an inward wish
You would desire the king were made a prelate.   40
Hear him debate of commonwealth affairs,
You would say it hath been all in all his study.
List his discourse of war, and you shall hear

22 **fair regard** kind consideration. 24 **courses . . . youth** N.
26 **mortified** killed. 28 **Consideration** reflection, spiritual contemplation. 29 **offending Adam** N. 33 **flood** N. 34 **heady currance**
headlong current. 35 **Hydra-headed** the Hydra was a many-
headed monster killed by Hercules. 36 **his seat** its power. 38
divinity theology. 43 **List** listen to.

A fearful battle rend'red you in music.
Turn him to any cause of policy,   45
The Gordian knot of it he will unloose,
Familiar as his garter; that, when he speaks,
The air, a charter'd libertine, is still,
And the mute wonder lurketh in men's ears
To steal his sweet and honey'd sentences.   50
So that the art and practic part of life
Must be the mistress to this theoric;
Which is a wonder how his grace should glean it,
Since his addiction was to courses vain,
His companies unletter'd, rude, and shallow,   55
His hours fill'd up with riots, banquets, sports,
And never noted in him any study,
Any retirement, any sequestration
From open haunts and popularity.   59
   Ely. The strawberry grows underneath the nettle,
And wholesome berries thrive and ripen best
Neighbor'd by fruit of baser quality.
And so the prince obscur'd his contemplation
Under the veil of wildness, which, no doubt,
Grew like the summer grass, fastest by night,   65
Unseen, yet crescive in his faculty.
   Canterbury. It must be so, for miracles are ceas'd,
And therefore we must needs admit the means
How things are perfected.

45 **cause of policy** problem of statecraft. 47 **Familiar as** though it
were as familiar. **that** so that. 48 **charter'd libertine** one privileged
to have freedom. 49 **wonder** wonderer. 50 **sentences** wise sayings.
51–2 **art . . . theoric** i.e. experience must have taught him theory.
54 **vain** idle. 55 **companies** companions. **rude** uncultivated. 58
sequestration withdrawal, seclusion. 59 **popularity** low company.
63 **contemplation** thoughtfulness. 64 **which** i.e. his contemplation.
66 **crescive . . . faculty** increasing in its natural power. 69 **perfected** stressed ´— — —́.

Ely.   But, my good lord,
How now for mitigation of this bill   70
Urg'd by the Commons? Doth his majesty
Incline to it, or no?
   Canterbury.   He seems indifferent,
Or rather swaying more upon our part
Than cherishing th' exhibiters against us.
For I have made an offer to his majesty,   75
Upon our spiritual convocation
And in regard of causes now in hand,
Which I have open'd to his grace at large,
As touching France, to give a greater sum
Than ever at one time the clergy yet   80
Did to his predecessors part withal.
   Ely. How did this offer seem receiv'd, my lord?
   Canterbury. With good acceptance of his majesty,
Save that there was not time enough to hear,
As I perceiv'd his grace would fain have done,   85
The severals and unhidden passages
Of his true titles to some certain dukedoms,
And generally to the crown and seat of France,
Deriv'd from Edward, his great-grandfather.   89
   Ely. What was th' impediment that broke this off?
   Canterbury. The French ambassador upon that instant
Crav'd audience, and the hour I think is come
To give him hearing. Is it four o'clock?
   Ely. It is.   94
   Canterbury. Then go we in to know his embassy,

---

72 **indifferent** impartial. 74 **exhibiters** i.e. those who sponsored
the bill in Parliament. 76 **Upon** as a result of. 77 **causes** issues.
78 **open'd . . . at large** set forth in full. 81 **withal** with. 86
severals . . . passages details and clear lines of descent. 88 **seat**
throne. 89 **Edward** N. 90 **impediment** interruption.

Which I could with a ready guess declare
Before the Frenchman speak a word of it.
  Ely. I'll wait upon you, and I long to hear it.
Exeunt.

SCENE 2

*Enter the King, Humphrey [Duke of Gloucester],
Bedford, Clarence, Warwick, Westmoreland, and
Exeter [with Attendants].*

King. Where is my gracious Lord of Canterbury?
Exeter. Not here in presence.
King.   Send for him, good uncle.
Westmoreland. Shall we call in th' ambassador, my
    liege?
King. Not yet, my cousin. We would be resolv'd
Before we hear him of some things of weight   5
That task our thoughts, concerning us and France.

*Enter two Bishops [the Archbishop of Canterbury
and the Bishop of Ely].*

Canterbury. God and his angels guard your sacred
    throne
And make you long become it!
King.   Sure we thank you.
My learned lord, we pray you to proceed
And justly and religiously unfold   10

SD **Clarence** does not speak, and appears here only. **Westmoreland** F *Westmerland* suggests pronunciation. (F refers throughout
to the First Folio of 1623, F2 to the Second Folio, etc.) 4 **cousin**
Westmoreland married Henry's cousin. 4–5 **resolv'd . . . of** satisfied about. 6 **task** trouble, occupy.

Why the law Salic that they have in France
Or should or should not bar us in our claim.
And God forbid, my dear and faithful lord,
That you should fashion, wrest, or bow your reading,
Or nicely charge your understanding soul   15
With opening titles miscreate, whose right
Suits not in native colors with the truth.
For God doth know how many now in health
Shall drop their blood in approbation
Of what your reverence shall incite us to.   20
Therefore take heed how you impawn our person,
How you awake our sleeping sword of war.
We charge you, in the name of God, take heed.
For never two such kingdoms did contend   24
Without much fall of blood, whose guiltless drops
Are every one a woe, a sore complaint
'Gainst him whose wrongs gives edge unto the swords
That makes such waste in brief mortality.
Under this conjuration, speak, my lord,
For we will hear, note, and believe in heart   30
That what you speak is in your conscience wash'd
As pure as sin with baptism.
   Canterbury. Then hear me, gracious sovereign, and
      you peers,
That owe yourselves, your lives, and services
To this imperial throne. There is no bar   35
To make against your highness' claim to France
But this which they produce from Pharamond:

11 law Salic N. 12 Or . . . or either . . . or. 15 nicely charge
burden with excessive ingenuity. 16 opening setting forth. miscreate falsely fabricated. 17 in . . . colors in their essential
nature. 19–20 in approbation Of in proving the justice of. 21
impawn pledge. 27 wrongs wrongful acts. 27–8 gives . . . makes
N. 28 mortality human life. 29 conjuration solemn appeal. 32 sin
original sin. 37 Pharamond legendary Frankish king.

In terram Salicam mulieres ne succedant—
'No woman shall succeed in Salic land.'
Which Salic land the French unjustly gloze   40
To be the realm of France, and Pharamond
The founder of this law and female bar.
Yet their own authors faithfully affirm
That the land Salic is in Germany,
Between the floods of Sala and of Elbe,   45
Where Charles the Great, having subdu'd the Saxons,
There left behind and settled certain French,
Who, holding in disdain the German women
For some dishonest manners of their life,
Establish'd then this law: to wit, no female   50
Should be inheritrix in Salic land.
Which Salic, as I said, 'twixt Elbe and Sala,
Is at this day in Germany call'd Meissen.
Then doth it well appear the Salic law
Was not devised for the realm of France,   55
Nor did the French possess the Salic land
Until four hundred one and twenty years
After defunction of King Pharamond,
Idly suppos'd the founder of this law,
Who died within the year of our redemption,   60
Four hundred twenty-six; and Charles the Great
Subdu'd the Saxons and did seat the French
Beyond the River Sala in the year
Eight hundred five. Besides, their writers say,
King Pepin, which deposed Childeric,   65
Did, as heir general, being descended
Of Blithild, which was daughter to King Clothair,
Make claim and title to the crown of France.

40 **gloze** gloss, interpret. 42 **female bar** bar against females.
46 **Charles the Great** Charlemagne N. 49 **dishonest** unchaste.
58 **defunction** death. 66 **heir general** male or female legal heir.

9

Hugh Capet also—who usurp'd the crown
Of Charles the Duke of Lorraine, sole heir male   70
Of the true line and stock of Charles the Great—
To find his title with some shows of truth,
Though in pure truth it was corrupt and naught,
Convey'd himself as th' heir to th' Lady Lingare,
Daughter to Charlemagne, who was the son   75
To Lewis the emperor, and Lewis the son
Of Charles the Great. Also King Lewis the Tenth,
Who was sole heir to the usurper Capet,
Could not keep quiet in his conscience,
Wearing the crown of France, till satisfied   80
That fair Queen Isabel, his grandmother,
Was lineal of the Lady Ermengare,
Daughter to Charles the foresaid Duke of Lorraine;
By which marriage the line of Charles the Great
Was reunited to the crown of France.   85
So that, as clear as is the summer's sun,
King Pepin's title and Hugh Capet's claim,
King Lewis his satisfaction, all appear
To hold in right and title of the female.
So do the kings of France unto this day,   90
Howbeit they would hold up this Salic law
To bar your highness claiming from the female,
And rather choose to hide them in a net
Than amply to imbare their crooked titles,

72 **find** provide; Q *fine*, furbish. (Q refers throughout to the First
Quarto of 1600, Q2 to the Second Quarto, etc.) **shows** appear-
ances. 74 **Convey'd** falsely represented. 75 **Charlemagne** historically Charles the Bald. 77 **Lewis the Tenth** read 'Lews' N. 79
conscience trisyllabic. 82 **lineal** direct descendant. 86–102 **So
that . . . ancestors** N. 88 **Lewis his** Lewis'. 93 **hide . . . net**
hide themselves in transparent deceits or contradictions. 94 **amply
to imbare** to lay bare completely N.

Usurp'd from you and your progenitors.   95
   King. May I with right and conscience make this
     claim?
   Canterbury. The sin upon my head, dread sov-
     ereign!
For in the Book of Numbers is it writ:
When the man dies, let the inheritance
Descend unto the daughter. Gracious lord,   100
Stand for your own, unwind your bloody flag,
Look back into your mighty ancestors.
Go, my dread lord, to your great-grandsire's tomb,
From whom you claim. Invoke his warlike spirit,
And your great-uncle's, Edward the Black Prince,
Who on the French ground play'd a tragedy,   106
Making defeat on the full power of France,
Whiles his most mighty father on a hill
Stood smiling to behold his lion's whelp
Forage in blood of French nobility.   110
O noble English, that could entertain
With half their forces the full pride of France
And let another half stand laughing by,
All out of work and cold for action!   114
   Ely. Awake remembrance of these valiant dead,
And with your puissant arm renew their feats.
You are their heir, you sit upon their throne.
The blood and courage that renowned them
Runs in your veins. And my thrice-puissant liege
Is in the very May morn of his youth,   120
Ripe for exploits and mighty enterprises.

98 **Numbers** see Numbers 27:8. 104 **claim** i.e. your right. 107
defeat destruction, at the Battle of Crécy, 1346. 110 **Forage in**
prey on. 111 **entertain** occupy. 114 **for** for want of. 116 **puissant**
powerful.

Exeter. Your brother kings and monarchs of the
  earth
Do all expect that you should rouse yourself,
As did the former lions of your blood.
  Westmoreland. They know your grace hath cause
    and means and might;   125
So hath your highness. Never King of England
Had nobles richer and more loyal subjects,
Whose hearts have left their bodies here in England
And lie pavilion'd in the fields of France.   129
  Canterbury. O, let their bodies follow, my dear liege,
With blood and sword and fire to win your right!
In aid whereof we of the spiritualty
Will raise your highness such a mighty sum
As never did the clergy at one time
Bring in to any of your ancestors.   135
  King. We must not only arm t' invade the French,
But lay down our proportions to defend
Against the Scot, who will make road upon us
With all advantages.
  Canterbury. They of those marches, gracious sov-
    ereign,   140
Shall be a wall sufficient to defend
Our inland from the pilfering borderers.
  King. We do not mean the coursing snatchers only,
But fear the main intendment of the Scot,
Who hath been still a giddy neighbor to us.   145
For you shall read that my great-grandfather
Never went with his forces into France

126 **hath** accented word. 129 **pavilion'd** encamped. 132 **spiritualty**
clergy (trisyllabic). 137 **lay . . . proportions** estimate the required number of troops. 138 **road** inroad. 139 **all advantages**
every favorable opportunity. 140 **marches** borders. 143 **coursing
snatchers** mounted raiders. 144 **intendment** intention. 145 **still**
always. **giddy** unstable.

But that the Scot on his unfurnish'd kingdom
Came pouring like the tide into a breach,
With ample and brim fullness of his force,　　　150
Galling the gleaned land with hot assays,
Girding with grievous siege castles and towns;
That England, being empty of defense,
Hath shook and trembled at th' ill neighborhood.
 Canterbury. She hath been then more fear'd than
  harm'd, my liege.　　　155
For hear her but exampled by herself:
When all her chivalry hath been in France
And she a mourning widow of her nobles,
She hath herself not only well defended
But taken and impounded as a stray　　　160
The King of Scots, whom she did send to France
To fill King Edward's fame with prisoner kings
And make her chronicle as rich with praise
As is the ooze and bottom of the sea
With sunken wrack and sumless treasuries.　　　165
 Ely. But there's a saying very old and true:
  'If that you will France win,
  Then with Scotland first begin.'
For once the eagle England being in prey,
To her unguarded nest the weasel Scot　　　170
Comes sneaking, and so sucks her princely eggs,
Playing the mouse in absence of the cat,
To tame and havoc more than she can eat.

148 **unfurnish'd** unprotected. 151 **Galling** blistering. **gleaned** stripped of its defenders. **assays** attacks. 153 **That** so that. 155 **fear'd** frightened. 156 **exampled by** setting a precedent for. 160 **impounded . . . stray** put in a pound like a stray animal. 161 **King of Scots** David Bruce. 163 **her** F *their*. 165 **wrack** wreck. **sumless** inestimable. 167 **France** probably dissyllabic. 169 **in prey** in search of prey. 173 **tame** broach, break into N. **havoc** destroy.

Exeter. It follows then the cat must stay at home.
Yet that is but a crush'd necessity,   175
Since we have locks to safeguard necessaries
And pretty traps to catch the petty thieves.
While that the armed hand doth fight abroad,
Th' advised head defends itself at home.   179
For government, though high and low and lower,
Put into parts, doth keep in one consent,
Congreeing in a full and natural close,
Like music.
   Canterbury. Therefore doth heaven divide
The state of man in divers functions,
Setting endeavor in continual motion,   185
To which is fixed as an aim or butt
Obedience. For so work the honeybees,
Creatures that by a rule in nature teach
The act of order to a peopled kingdom.
They have a king, and officers of sorts,   190
Where some like magistrates correct at home,
Others like merchants venter trade abroad,
Others like soldiers armed in their stings
Make boot upon the summer's velvet buds,
Which pillage they with merry march bring home 195
To the tent royal of their emperor;
Who, busied in his majesty, surveys
The singing masons building roofs of gold,

174 then F *theu.* 175 crush'd forced; Q *curst.* 177 pretty good,
ingenious; may rhyme with *petty.* 179 advised thoughtful. 181–2
parts . . . close terms referring to both government and music.
181 consent harmony (cf. 'concent'). 182 Congreeing agreeing,
harmonizing. natural read 'nat'ral.' close cadence. 184 state of
man human life. 186 butt end, target. 187 honeybees N. 188 rule
precept. 189 act operation. 190 sorts various ranks. 191 correct
inflict punishment. 192 venter trade venture upon, speculate in
trade. 194 Make . . . upon plunder.

The civil citizens kneading up the honey,
The poor mechanic porters crowding in   200
Their heavy burthens at his narrow gate,
The sad-ey'd justice with his surly hum,
Delivering o'er to executors pale
The lazy yawning drone. I this infer,
That many things having full reference   205
To one consent may work contrariously:
As many arrows loosed several ways
Come to one mark; as many ways meet in one town;
As many fresh streams meet in one salt sea;
As many lines close in the dial's center—   210
So may a thousand actions, once afoot,
End in one purpose, and be all well borne
Without defeat. Therefore to France, my liege!
Divide your happy England into four,
Whereof take you one quarter into France,   215
And you withal shall make all Gallia shake.
If we with thrice such powers left at home
Cannot defend our own doors from the dog,
Let us be worried and our nation lose
The name of hardiness and policy.   220
  King. Call in the messengers sent from the Dolphin.
      [Exeunt some Attendants.]
Now are we well resolv'd, and by God's help
And yours, the noble sinews of our power,
France being ours, we'll bend it to our awe
Or break it all to pieces. Or there we'll sit,   225
Ruling in large and ample empery

199 **civil** well-behaved. 202 **sad-ey'd** sober-looking. 203 **executors**
executioners; stressed $\stackrel{\smile}{-} - - \stackrel{\smile}{-} -$. 207 **loosed . . . ways** shot
from different directions. 210 **dial's** sundial's. 212 **End** Q; F *And*.
borne carried out. 216 **withal** therewith. **Gallia** Latin name for
France. 217 **powers** forces. 220 **policy** statesmanship. 221 **Dolphin**
Dauphin N. 225 **Or** either. 226 **empery** sovereignty.

O'er France and all her almost kingly dukedoms,
Or lay these bones in an unworthy urn,
Tombless, with no remembrance over them.
Either our history shall with full mouth   230
Speak freely of our acts, or else our grave,
Like Turkish mute, shall have a tongueless mouth,
Not worship'd with a waxen epitaph.

Enter Ambassadors of France.

Now are we well prepar'd to know the pleasure
Of our fair cousin Dolphin, for we hear   235
Your greeting is from him, not from the king.
   Ambassador. May't please your majesty to give us
      leave
Freely to render what we have in charge,
Or shall we sparingly show you far off
The Dolphin's meaning and our embassy?   240
   King. We are no tyrant, but a Christian king,
Unto whose grace our passion is as subject
As is our wretches fett'red in our prisons.
Therefore with frank and with uncurbed plainness
Tell us the Dolphin's mind.
   Ambassador.   Thus then, in few: 245
Your highness, lately sending into France,
Did claim some certain dukedoms in the right
Of your great predecessor, King Edward the Third.
In answer of which claim, the prince our master
Says that you savor too much of your youth,   250
And bids you be advis'd. There's nought in France
That can be with a nimble galliard won.

228 **urn** grave. 232 **Turkish mute** N. 233 **worship'd** honored.
with . . . epitaph even with an epitaph made out of wax. 238
render report. 242 **grace** merciful disposition. 243 **is** see I. Pro. 9
N. 245 **in few** in brief. 251 **be advis'd** consider. 252 **galliard**
a lively dance.

You cannot revel into dukedoms there.
He therefore sends you, meeter for your spirit,
This tun of treasure, and, in lieu of this,   255
Desires you let the dukedoms that you claim
Hear no more of you. This the Dolphin speaks.
  King. What treasure, uncle?
  Exeter.   Tennis balls, my liege.
  King. We are glad the Dolphin is so pleasant with
      us.
His present and your pains we thank you for.   260
When we have match'd our rackets to these balls,
We will in France, by God's grace, play a set
Shall strike his father's crown into the hazard.
Tell him he hath made a match with such a wrangler
That all the courts of France will be disturb'd   265
With chases. And we understand him well,
How he comes o'er us with our wilder days,
Not measuring what use we made of them.
We never valu'd this poor seat of England,
And therefore, living hence, did give ourself   270
To barbarous license, as 'tis ever common
That men are merriest when they are from home.
But tell the Dolphin I will keep my state,
Be like a king, and show my sail of greatness,
When I do rouse me in my throne of France.   275
For that I have laid by my majesty
And plodded like a man for working days.
But I will rise there with so full a glory
That I will dazzle all the eyes of France—

254 meeter more fitting. 255 tun cask. in lieu of in return for.
258–66 Tennis . . . chases N. 259 pleasant facetious. 262–6
set . . . chases N. 264 he hath read 'he'th.' 267 comes o'er
taunts. 269 seat throne. 270 hence away from the court. 273
state chair of state, dignity. 276 For that to that end.

Yea, strike the Dolphin blind to look on us. 280
And tell the pleasant prince this mock of his
Hath turn'd his balls to gunstones, and his soul
Shall stand sore charged for the wasteful vengeance
That shall fly with them. For many a thousand
    widows 284
Shall this his mock mock out of their dear husbands,
Mock mothers from their sons, mock castles down.
And some are yet ungotten and unborn
That shall have cause to curse the Dolphin's scorn.
But this lies all within the will of God,
To whom I do appeal and in whose name, 290
Tell you the Dolphin, I am coming on,
To venge me as I may and to put forth
My rightful hand in a well-hallow'd cause.
So get you hence in peace. And tell the Dolphin
His jest will savor but of shallow wit 295
When thousands weep more than did laugh at it.
Convey them with safe conduct. Fare you well.
                    Exeunt Ambassadors.
  Exeter. This was a merry message.
  King. We hope to make the sender blush at it.
Therefore, my lords, omit no happy hour 300
That may give furth'rance to our expedition.
For we have now no thought in us but France,
Save those to God, that run before our business.
Therefore let our proportions for these wars
Be soon collected, and all things thought upon 305
That may with reasonable swiftness add

---

282 **gunstones** cannon balls, originally made of stone. 283 **wasteful** devastating. 287 **ungotten** unbegotten. 292 **venge me** avenge myself. 297 **Convey** escort. 300 **omit** neglect. **happy** favorable. 304 **proportions** forces.

More feathers to our wings. For, God before,
We'll chide this Dolphin at his father's door.
Therefore let every man now task his thought,
That this fair action may on foot be brought.   310
                                        Exeunt.

307 **God before** God leading us. 309 **task his thought** take careful
thought.

Act II

Flourish. Enter Chorus.

Now all the youth of England are on fire,
And silken dalliance in the wardrobe lies.
Now thrive the armorers, and honor's thought
Reigns solely in the breast of every man.
They sell the pasture now to buy the horse,   5
Following the mirror of all Christian kings
With winged heels, as English Mercuries.
For now sits Expectation in the air
And hides a sword from hilts unto the point
With crowns imperial, crowns and coronets,   10
Promis'd to Harry and his followers.
The French, advis'd by good intelligence
Of this most dreadful preparation,
Shake in their fear and with pale policy
Seek to divert the English purposes.   15
O England! model to thy inward greatness,
Like little body with a mighty heart,
What mightst thou do that honor would thee do,
Were all thy children kind and natural!   19
But see, thy fault France hath in thee found out,

SD **Flourish** music of trumpets N. 2 **silken dalliance** the clothes
and manners of society. 6 **mirror** perfect pattern. 7 **winged** . . .
Mercuries N. 9 **hilts** crosspiece protecting the handle. 12 **intelligence** espionage. 14 **pale policy** diplomacy directed by fear.
16 **model to** small replica of. 18 **would thee do** would have thee do.
19 **kind** showing filial love. 20 **see** . . . **hath** many editors read
'see thy fault! France hath.' **France** King of France.

A nest of hollow bosoms, which he fills
With treacherous crowns. And three corrupted
    men—
One, Richard Earl of Cambridge, and the second,
Henry Lord Scroop of Masham, and the third,   24
Sir Thomas Grey, knight, of Northumberland—
Have, for the gilt of France—O, guilt indeed!—
Confirm'd conspiracy with fearful France.
And by their hands this grace of kings must die,
If hell and treason hold their promises,   29
Ere he take ship for France, and in Southampton.
Linger your patience on, and we'll digest
Th' abuse of distance, force a play.
The sum is paid, the traitors are agreed,
The king is set from London, and the scene
Is now transported, gentles, to Southampton.   35
There is the playhouse now, there must you sit,
And thence to France shall we convey you safe
And bring you back, charming the narrow seas
To give you gentle pass. For, if we may,
We'll not offend one stomach with our play.   40
But till the king come forth, and not till then,
Unto Southampton do we shift our scene.   *Exit.*

---

22 **crowns** crown pieces, gold. 26 **gilt . . . guilt** common pun in
Shakespeare, *gilt* meaning 'gold.' 28 **grace of kings** one who dig-
nifies the role of kingship. 31–2 **digest . . . abuse** overcome the
problem. 32 **force** stuff out, or make a play in spite of difficulties.
39 **pass** passage. 39–40 **For . . . play** N. 39 **may** can help it.
40 **offend one stomach** offend anyone's taste, or make anyone
seasick. 41–2 **But . . . scene** the scene will be shifted to Southampton when the king comes forth (scene 2).

SCENE 1

Enter Corporal Nym and Lieutenant Bardolph.

Bardolph. Well met, Corporal Nym.

Nym. Good morrow, Lieutenant Bardolph.

Bardolph. What, are Ancient Pistol and you friends
yet? 4

Nym. For my part, I care not. I say little. But
when time shall serve, there shall be smiles—but that
shall be as it may. I dare not fight, but I will wink
and hold out mine iron. It is a simple one, but what
though? It will toast cheese, and it will endure cold,
as another man's sword will, and there's an end.

Bardolph. I will bestow a breakfast to make you
friends, and we'll be all three sworn brothers to
France. Let't be so, good Corporal Nym. 13

Nym. Faith, I will live so long as I may, that's the
certain of it. And when I cannot live any longer, I
will do as I may. That is my rest, that is the rendezvous of it.

Bardolph. It is certain, corporal, that he is married to Nell Quickly, and certainly she did you
wrong, for you were trothplight to her. 20

Nym. I cannot tell. Things must be as they may.
Men may sleep, and they may have their throats
about them at that time, and some say knives have

1 **Nym** the name means 'steal' and 'thief.' 3 **Ancient** ensign,
second lieutenant. 7 **wink** keep my eyes closed. 8 **iron** sword.
12 **sworn brothers** comical allusion to knightly brethren in arms.
14 **may** can. 16 **rest** resolve. 16–7 **rendezvous** refuge, last resort.
19 **Nell Quickly** N. 20 **trothplight** formally bethrothed.

edges. It must be as it may. Though patience be a
tired mare, yet she will plod. There must be conclu-
sions. Well, I cannot tell.   26

Enter Pistol and [Hostess] Quickly.

Bardolph. Here comes Ancient Pistol and his wife.
Good corporal, be patient here. How now, mine host
Pistol?

Pistol. Base tyke, call'st thou me host?   30
Now by this hand I swear I scorn the term,
Nor shall my Nell keep lodgers.

Hostess. No, by my troth, not long. For we cannot
lodge and board a dozen or fourteen gentlewomen
that live honestly by the prick of their needles, but
it will be thought we keep a bawdy house straight.
[*Nym and Pistol draw.*] O welladay, Lady! If he be
not hewn now, we shall see willful adultery and murther committed.   39

Bardolph. Good lieutenant! Good corporal! Offer
nothing here.

Nym. Pish!

Pistol. Pish for thee, Iceland dog! Thou prick-ear'd
cur of Iceland!   44

Hostess. Good Corporal Nym, show thy valor, and
put up your sword.

Nym. Will you shog off? I would have you solus.

Pistol. 'Solus,' egregious dog? O viper vile!

24–5 **Though . . . plod** N. 25 **mare** Q; F *name*. 30 **tyke** cur N.
host tavernkeeper. 35 **honestly** chastely. 37 **Nym . . . draw**
perhaps only Nym draws here. **welladay** wellaway. 37 **Lady** by
Our Lady. 38 **hewn** cut down; many editors read *drawn*. 43–4
Iceland . . . cur lap dogs with sharp erect ears. 47 **shog off**
move off. **solus** alone (Pistol thinks it an insult and rants like a
conjuror). 48 **egregious** in the highest degree.

The 'solus' in thy most mervailous face,
The 'solus' in thy teeth, and in thy throat,   50
And in thy hateful lungs—yea, in thy maw, perdy,
And, which is worse, within thy nasty mouth!
I do retort the 'solus' in thy bowels,
For I can take, and Pistol's cock is up,
And flashing fire will follow.   55

Nym. I am not Barbason; you cannot conjure me.
I have an humor to knock you indifferently well. If
you grow foul with me, Pistol, I will scour you with
my rapier, as I may, in fair terms. If you would
walk off, I would prick your guts a little, in good
terms, as I may, and that's the humor of it.

Pistol. O braggart vile, and damned furious wight!
The grave doth gape and doting death is near.
Therefore exhale.   64

Bardolph. Hear me, hear me what I say. He that
strikes the first stroke, I'll run him up to the hilts,
as I am a soldier.   [*Draws.*]

Pistol. An oath of mickle might, and fury shall
    abate.
Give me thy fist, thy forefoot to me give.
Thy spirits are most tall.   70

Nym. I will cut thy throat one time or other in fair
terms, that is the humor of it.

Pistol. 'Couple a gorge!'

---

49 **mervailous** marvelous; here stressed — ´ —. 51 **maw** stomach.
perdy by God, indeed. 54 **take** strike; catch fire; bewitch. Pistol's
cock lever on a gun N. 56 **I am . . . me** I cannot be called up
and dismissed like a fiend. 57 **indifferently** fairly. 58 **scour** thrash;
clean out a pistol. 59 **in fair terms** in good style. 61 **humor** N.
64 **exhale** draw your sword; die. 67 **Draws** Q *They drawe.* 68
mickle great. 70 **tall** courageous. 73 **Couple a gorge** Pistol's French
for *couper la gorge*, 'to cut the throat.'

That is the word. I thee defy again.   74
O hound of Crete, think'st thou my spouse to get?
No, to the spital go,
And from the powd'ring tub of infamy
Fetch forth the lazar kite of Cressid's kind,
Doll Tearsheet, she by name, and her espouse.
I have, and I will hold, the quondam Quickly   80
For the only she, and—pauca, there's enough.
Go to!

Enter the Boy.

Boy. Mine host Pistol, you must come to my master,
and your hostess. He is very sick and would to bed.
Good Bardolph, put thy face between his sheets and
do the office of a warming pan. Faith, he's very ill.

Bardolph. Away, you rogue!   87

Hostess. By my troth, he'll yield the crow a pudding
one of these days. The king has kill'd his heart. Good
husband, come home presently.   *Exit* [*with Boy*].

Bardolph. Come, shall I make you two friends? We
must to France together. Why the divel should we
keep knives to cut one another's throats?

Pistol. Let floods o'erswell, and fiends for food howl
on!   94

Nym. You'll pay me the eight shillings I won of you
at betting?

Pistol. Base is the slave that pays.

74 **thee defy** Q; F *defie thee.* 76–9 **No . . . espouse** N. 76 **spital**
hospital. 77 **powd'ring tub** i.e. for curing venereal diseases by
sweating. 78 **lazar . . . kind** N. 80 **quondam** former (now Mistress Pistol). 81 **only she** only woman for me. **pauca** in few words.
81–2 **enough. Go to** F *enough to go to.* 84 **your** many editors read
you,. 85–6 **face . . . pan** N. 88 **he'll . . . pudding** the boy will
be hanged and devoured by crows (proverbial). 89 **kill'd his
heart** N. 90 **presently** immediately. 92 **divel** N.

Nym. That now I will have. That's the humor of it.

Pistol. As manhood shall compound. Push home.

[They] draw.

Bardolph. By this sword, he that makes the first
thrust, I'll kill him! By this sword, I will.   101

Pistol. 'Sword' is an oath, and oaths must have
their course.

Bardolph. Corporal Nym, an thou wilt be friends,
be friends. An thou wilt not, why then be enemies
with me too. Prithee put up.   105

[*Nym.* I shall have my eight shillings I won of you
at betting?]

Pistol. A noble shalt thou have, and present pay,
And liquor likewise will I give to thee,
And friendship shall combine, and brotherhood.   110
I'll live by Nym, and Nym shall live by me.
Is not this just? For I shall sutler be
Unto the camp, and profits will accrue.
Give me thy hand.

Nym. I shall have my noble?   115

Pistol. In cash, most justly paid.

Nym. Well then, that's the humor of't.

Enter Hostess.

Hostess. As ever you come of women, come in
quickly to Sir John. Ah, poor heart! he is so shak'd
of a burning quotidian tertian that it is most lam-
entable to behold. Sweet men, come to him.   121

Nym. The king hath run bad humors on the knight,
that's the even of it.

99 **compound** come to terms. 103 **an** if; F (frequently) &. 105
put up sheathe your sword. 106–7 **I . . . betting** Q; not in F.
108 **noble** N. 111 **by Nym** i.e. by thievery. 112 **sutler** one who sells
provisions and liquor to an army. 117 **that's** F *that*. 120 **quotidian
tertian** N. 122 **run . . . humors** vented his ill humor.

Pistol. Nym, thou hast spoke the right.
His heart is fracted and corroborate.   125
    Nym. The king is a good king, but it must be as it
may. He passes some humors and careers.
    Pistol. Let us condole the knight, for, lambkins, we
will live.   [*Exeunt.*]

SCENE 2

Enter Exeter, Bedford, and Westmoreland.

Bedford. 'Fore God, his grace is bold to trust these
        traitors.
Exeter. They shall be apprehended by and by.
Westmoreland. How smooth and even they do bear
        themselves,
As if allegiance in their bosoms sat,
Crowned with faith and constant loyalty!   5
    Bedford. The king hath note of all that they intend,
By interception which they dream not of.
    Exeter. Nay, but the man that was his bedfellow,
Whom he hath dull'd and cloy'd with gracious fa-
        vors—
That he should for a foreign purse so sell   10
His sovereign's life to death and treachery!

*Sound trumpets. Enter the King, Scroop, Cambridge,
        and Grey [with Attendants].*

    King. Now sits the wind fair, and we will aboard.

---

125 **fracted** broken N. 127 **passes . . . careers** N. 2 **apprehended
. . . by** arrested very soon. 7 **interception** i.e. by intercepting
their communications. 8 **bedfellow** bosom friend (Scroop).

My Lord of Cambridge, and my kind Lord of Ma-
sham,
And you, my gentle knight, give me your thoughts.
Think you not that the pow'rs we bear with us   15
Will cut their passage through the force of France,
Doing the execution and the act
For which we have in head assembled them?

  Scroop. No doubt, my liege, if each man do his best.

  King. I doubt not that, since we are well persuaded
We carry not a heart with us from hence   21
That grows not in a fair consent with ours,
Nor leave not one behind that doth not wish
Success and conquest to attend on us.

  Cambridge. Never was monarch better fear'd and
lov'd   25
Than is your majesty. There's not, I think, a subject
That sits in heart-grief and uneasiness
Under the sweet shade of your government.

  Grey. True. Those that were your father's enemies
Have steep'd their galls in honey and do serve you
With hearts create of duty and of zeal.   31

  King. We therefore have great cause of thank-
fulness
And shall forget the office of our hand
Sooner than quittance of desert and merit
According to the weight and worthiness.   35

  Scroop. So service shall with steeled sinews toil,
And labor shall refresh itself with hope
To do your grace incessant services.

  King. We judge no less. Uncle of Exeter,

15 pow'rs forces; F *powres.* 18 **in head** in an armed force. 22
grows . . . consent is not in agreement. 29 Grey F *Kni* [ght].
30 **galls** bitterness, resentment. 31 **create** made. 33 **office** use.
34 **quittance of** recompense for.

Enlarge the man committed yesterday   40
That rail'd against our person. We consider
It was excess of wine that set him on,
And on his more advice we pardon him.
  Scroop. That's mercy, but too much security.
Let him be punish'd, sovereign, lest example   45
Breed, by his sufferance, more of such a kind.
  King. O, let us yet be merciful!
  Cambridge. So may your highness, and yet punish
    too.
  Grey. Sir,
You show great mercy if you give him life,   50
After the taste of much correction.
  King. Alas, your too much love and care of me
Are heavy orisons 'gainst this poor wretch!
If little faults, proceeding on distemper,   54
Shall not be wink'd at, how shall we stretch our eye
When capital crimes, chew'd, swallow'd, and digested,
Appear before us? We'll yet enlarge that man,
Though Cambridge, Scroop, and Grey, in their dear
    care
And tender preservation of our person,
Would have him punish'd. And now to our French
    causes.   60
Who are the late commissioners?
  Cambridge. I one, my lord.
Your highness bade me ask for it today.

40 **Enlarge** release 43 **his more advice** his thinking better of it,
or our further consideration about him. 44 **security** carelessness,
overconfidence. 46 **his sufferance** i.e. letting him go without
punishment. 49 Sir F prints with l. 50. 53 **orisons** prayers. 54
distemper i.e. drunkenness. 55 **wink'd at** overlooked. **stretch our
eye** open our eyes sufficiently wide. 57 **yet** nevertheless. 61 **late**
lately appointed. 63 **it** i.e. an appointment as commissioner.

Scroop. So did you me, my liege.

Grey. And I, my royal sovereign.   65

King. Then, Richard Earl of Cambridge, there is yours,

There yours, Lord Scroop of Masham, and, Sir Knight,

Grey of Northumberland, this same is yours.

Read them, and know I know your worthiness.

My Lord of Westmoreland and Uncle Exeter,   70

We will aboard tonight. Why, how now, gentlemen!

What see you in those papers that you lose

So much complexion? Look ye how they change!

Their cheeks are paper. Why, what read you there,

That have so cowarded and chas'd your blood   75

Out of appearance?

Cambridge.   I do confess my fault,

And do submit me to your highness' mercy.

Grey, Scroop. To which we all appeal.

King. The mercy that was quick in us but late

By your own counsel is suppress'd and kill'd.   80

You must not dare, for shame, to talk of mercy,

For your own reasons turn into your bosoms

As dogs upon their masters, worrying you.

See you, my princes and my noble peers,

These English monsters! My Lord of Cambridge here,   85

You know how apt our love was to accord

To furnish him with all appertinents

Belonging to his honor. And this man

Hath, for a few light crowns, lightly conspir'd

And sworn unto the practices of France   90

---

79 **quick** alive. 82 **reasons** arguments. 86 **accord** consent. 87 **him** F2; not in F. **appertinents** appurtenances. 89 **lightly** thoughtlessly, easily. 90 **practices** plots.

To kill us here in Hampton. To the which
This knight, no less for bounty bound to us
Than Cambridge is, hath likewise sworn. But O,
What shall I say to thee, Lord Scroop—thou cruel,
Ingrateful, savage, and inhuman creature?   95
Thou that didst bear the key of all my counsels,
That knew'st the very bottom of my soul,
That almost mightst have coin'd me into gold—
Wouldst thou have practic'd on me for thy use?
May it be possible that foreign hire   100
Could out of thee extract one spark of evil
That might annoy my finger? 'Tis so strange
That, though the truth of it stands off as gross
As black and white, my eye will scarcely see it.
Treason and murther ever kept together,   105
As two yoke-divels sworn to either's purpose,
Working so grossly in a natural cause
That admiration did not whoop at them.
But thou, 'gainst all proportion, didst bring in
Wonder to wait on treason and on murther.   110
And whatsoever cunning fiend it was
That wrought upon thee so preposterously
Hath got the voice in hell for excellence.
All other divels that suggest by treasons
Do botch and bungle up damnation   115
With patches, colors, and with forms being fetch'd

91 Hampton Southampton. 92 for bounty i.e. for our bounty to
him. 96 counsels secrets. 99 practic'd . . . use used me for your
own purposes (Scroop had been treasurer). 100 May can. 102
annoy my finger hurt even my finger. 103 gross obvious, flagrant.
107 Working . . . cause working together so obviously in a cause
natural for them. 108 admiration wonder. whoop cry out; F
hoope. 109 proportion natural order. 112 preposterously mon-
strously, unnaturally. 113 voice vote. 114 All F And. 114–17
suggest . . . piety N.

From glist'ring semblances of piety.
But he that temper'd thee bade thee stand up,
Gave thee no instance why thou shouldst do treason,
Unless to dub thee with the name of traitor.   120
If that same demon that hath gull'd thee thus
Should with his lion gait walk the whole world,
He might return to vasty Tartar back
And tell the legions 'I can never win
A soul so easy as that Englishman's.'   125
O, how hast thou with jealousy infected
The sweetness of affiance! Show men dutiful?
Why, so didst thou. Seem they grave and learned?
Why, so didst thou. Come they of noble family?
Why, so didst thou. Seem they religious?   130
Why, so didst thou. Or are they spare in diet,
Free from gross passion or of mirth or anger,
Constant in spirit, not swerving with the blood,
Garnish'd and deck'd in modest complement,
Not working with the eye without the ear,   135
And but in purged judgment trusting neither?
Such and so finely bolted didst thou seem.
And thus thy fall hath left a kind of blot
To mark the full-fraught man and best indu'd
With some suspicion. I will weep for thee.   140
For this revolt of thine, methinks, is like

118 **temper'd** molded. **stand up** i.e. take up treason boldly. 120
dub confer knighthood upon (ironical). 121 **gull'd** deceived. 122
lion gait see 1 Peter 5:8. 123 **Tartar** Tartarus, hell. 126 **jealousy**
suspicion. 127 **affiance** trust, allegiance. **Show** appear. 127–40
Show . . . suspicion N. 130 **religious** (four syllables). 132 **or**
. . . or either . . . or. 133 **blood** passions. 134 **modest comple-**
ment outward appearance of modesty. 136 **purged** free from whim
or partiality. 137 **bolted** sifted, like flower from bran. 139 **mark**
the F *make thee.* **full-fraught** fully furnished. **indu'd** endowed.
32

Another fall of man. Their faults are open.
Arrest them to the answer of the law,
And God acquit them of their practices!　　144
　Exeter. I arrest thee of high treason, by the name
of Richard Earl of Cambridge.
I arrest thee of high treason, by the name of Henry
Lord Scroop of Masham.
I arrest thee of high treason, by the name of Thomas
Grey, knight, of Northumberland.　　150
　Scroop. Our purposes God justly hath discover'd,
And I repent my fault more than my death,
Which I beseech your highness to forgive,
Although my body pay the price of it.
　Cambridge. For me, the gold of France did not
　　seduce,　　155
Although I did admit it as a motive,
The sooner to effect what I intended.
But God be thanked for prevention,
Which I in sufferance heartily will rejoice,
Beseeching God and you to pardon me.　　160
　Grey. Never did faithful subject more rejoice
At the discovery of most dangerous treason
Than I do at this hour joy o'er myself,
Prevented from a damned enterprise.
My fault, but not my body, pardon, sovereign.　　165
　King. God quit you in his mercy! Hear your sen-
　　tence.
You have conspir'd against our royal person,
Join'd with an enemy proclaim'd, and from his cof-
fers

147 **Henry** Q; F *Thomas.* 148 **Masham** F *Marsham.* 158 **prevention** forestallment (four syllables). 159 **I** F2; not in F. **sufferance** suffering (death) N. 166 **quit** absolve. 167–81 **You have . . .** hence N.

Receiv'd the golden earnest of our death.   169
Wherein you would have sold your king to slaughter,
His princes and his peers to servitude,
His subjects to oppression and contempt,
And his whole kingdom into desolation.
Touching our person, seek we no revenge,
But we our kingdom's safety must so tender,   175
Whose ruin you have sought, that to her laws
We do deliver you. Get you therefore hence,
Poor miserable wretches, to your death,
The taste whereof God of his mercy give
You patience to endure and true repentance   180
Of all your dear offenses! Bear them hence.
    Exeunt [*Scroop, Cambridge, and Grey, guarded*].
Now, lords, for France, the enterprise whereof
Shall be to you as us, like glorious.
We doubt not of a fair and lucky war,
Since God so graciously hath brought to light   185
This dangerous treason lurking in our way
To hinder our beginnings. We doubt not now
But every rub is smoothed on our way.
Then forth, dear countrymen. Let us deliver
Our puissance into the hand of God,   190
Putting it straight in expedition.
Cheerly to sea, the signs of war advance!
No King of England, if not King of France!
                    Flourish. [*Exeunt.*]

169 **earnest** partial payment given on account of services to be rendered. 175 **tender** cherish. 176 **have** Q; not in F. 181 **dear** often an intensive, 'serious.' 183 **like** alike. 184 **fair** fortunate. 188 **rub** obstacle (figure from bowling). 190 **puissance** forces (trisyllabic). 191 **straight in expedition** immediately in motion. **expedition** five syllables. 192 **signs** standards.

SCENE 3

Enter Pistol, Nym, Bardolph, Boy, and Hostess.

Hostess. Prithee, honey-sweet husband, let me bring thee to Staines.

Pistol. No, for my manly heart doth earn.
Bardolph, be blithe. Nym, rouse thy vaunting veins.
Boy, bristle thy courage up; for Falstaff he is dead,
And we must earn therefore.   6

Bardolph. Would I were with him, wheresome'er he is, either in heaven or in hell!

Hostess. Nay, sure, he's not in hell. He's in Arthur's bosom, if ever man went to Arthur's bosom. A' made a finer end, and went away an it had been any christome child. A' parted ev'n just between twelve and one, ev'n at the turning o' th' tide. For after I saw him fumble with the sheets, and play with flowers, and smile upon his finger's end, I knew there was but one way. For his nose was as sharp as a pen, and a' babbled of green fields. 'How now, Sir John!' quoth I. 'What, man! Be o' good cheer.' So a' cried out 'God, God, God!' three or four times. Now I, to comfort him, bid him a' should not think of God; I hop'd there was no need to trouble himself with any such thoughts yet. So a' bade me lay more clothes on his feet. I put my hand into the bed and felt them, and

2 **Staines** commonly the first stop on the road to Southampton.
3–6 **No . . . therefore** F prints this and ll. 47–56 as prose.
3 **earn** grieve. 9–10 **Arthur's bosom** the Hostess mistakes Arthur's bosom for Abraham's (heaven); see Luke 16:22. 10 **A'** he N.
11 **an** as if. 11–12 **christome** chrisom, just christened, entirely innocent N. 15 **finger's end** F *fingers end;* most editors **read** *fingers' end* or *ends* (Q). 17 **a' babbled . . . fields** N.

they were as cold as any stone. Then I felt to his knees, and so upward and upward, and all was as cold as any stone. 26

Nym. They say he cried out of sack.

Hostess. Ay, that a' did.

Bardolph. And of women.

Hostess. Nay, that a' did not. 30

Boy. Yes, that a' did, and said they were devils incarnate.

Hostess. A' could never abide carnation. 'Twas a color he never lik'd. 34

Boy. A' said once the devil would have him about women.

Hostess. A' did in some sort, indeed, handle women; but then he was rheumatic, and talk'd of the whore of Babylon. 39

Boy. Do you not remember a' saw a flea stick upon Bardolph's nose, and a' said it was a black soul burning in hell?

Bardolph. Well, the fuel is gone that maintain'd that fire. That's all the riches I got in his service.

Nym. Shall we shog? The king will be gone from Southampton. 46

Pistol. Come, let's away. My love, give me thy lips. Look to my chattels and my movables. Let senses rule. The word is 'Pitch and pay.'

25 **knees** Q adds 'and they were as cold as any stone.' **upward** F *vp-peer'd, and vpward,* suggests pronunciation. 27 **of** against. **sack** a white wine N. 38 **rheumatic** probably she means 'lunatic'; F *rumatique;* stressed ́— — —. 38–9 **whore of Babylon** the 'scarlet woman' of Revelations 17; the Church of Rome (Romeatic). 45 **shog** move on. 48 **movables** furniture, possessions. 49 **senses** common sense. **word** Q; F *world.* **Pitch and pay** i.e. cash down.

Trust none;   50
For oaths are straws, men's faiths are wafer cakes,
And hold-fast is the only dog, my duck.
Therefore Caveto be thy counselor.
Go, clear thy crystals. Yoke-fellows in arms,
Let us to France, like horseleeches, my boys,   55
To suck, to suck, the very blood to suck!
  Boy. And that's but unwholesome food, they say.
  Pistol. Touch her soft mouth, and march.
  Bardolph. Farwell, Hostess.   [*Kissing her.*]
  Nym. I cannot kiss, that is the humor of it. But
adieu.   61
  Pistol. Let huswifery appear. Keep close, I thee
command.
  Hostess. Farewell, adieu.   *Exeunt.*

SCENE 4

Flourish. Enter the French King, the Dolphin, the
Dukes of Berri and Britaine[, *the Constable, and*
others].

  King. Thus comes the English with full pow'r upon
        us,
And more than carefully it us concerns
To answer royally in our defenses.
Therefore the Dukes of Berri and of Britaine,
Of Brabant and of Orleans, shall make forth,   5

52 **hold-fast** from the old proverb 'Brag is a good dog, but
Hold-fast is better.' 53 **Caveto** caution; Q *cophetua.* 54 **crystals**
eyes. 59 **Farwell** farewell. 62 **huswifery** housewifery, good management (pronounced 'húzzifry'). **Keep close** stay at home.
SD **Flourish** trumpet fanfare. **Constable** here the chief military
officer of France.

And you, Prince Dolphin, with all swift dispatch,
To line and new repair our towns of war
With men of courage and with means defendant.
For England his approaches makes as fierce
As waters to the sucking of a gulf.   10
It fits us then to be as provident
As fear may teach us out of late examples
Left by the fatal and neglected English
Upon our fields.
   Dolphin.   My most redoubted father,
It is most meet we arm us 'gainst the foe,   15
For peace itself should not so dull a kingdom,
Though war nor no known quarrel were in question,
But that defenses, musters, preparations
Should be maintain'd, assembled, and collected
As were a war in expectation.   20
Therefore I say 'tis meet we all go forth
To view the sick and feeble parts of France.
And let us do it with no show of fear—
No, with no more than if we heard that England
Were busied with a Whitsun morris dance.   25
For, my good liege, she is so idly king'd,
Her scepter so fantastically borne,
By a vain, giddy, shallow, humorous youth,
That fear attends her not.
   Constable.   O, peace, Prince Dolphin!
You are too much mistaken in this king.   30
Question your grace the late ambassadors,
With what great state he heard their embassy,

7 **line** strengthen. 8 **means defendant** means of defense. 10 **gulf**
whirlpool. 12 **late examples** battles at Crécy and Poitiers. See
ll. 53–64 below. 13 **fatal and neglected** fatally underrated. 14
redoubted feared. 20 **expectation** five syllables. 25 **Whitsun . . .
dance** N. 26 **idly king'd** i.e. has so frivolous a king. 28 **humorous**
capricious.

How well supplied with noble councilors,
How modest in exception, and withal
How terrible in constant resolution, 35
And you shall find his vanities forespent
Were but the outside of the Roman Brutus,
Covering discretion with a coat of folly,
As gardeners do with ordure hide those roots
That shall first spring and be most delicate. 40
    Dolphin. Well, 'tis not so, my Lord High Constable,
But though we think it so, it is no matter.
In cases of defense 'tis best to weigh
The enemy more mighty than he seems.
So the proportions of defense are fill'd, 45
Which of a weak and niggardly projection
Doth like a miser spoil his coat with scanting
A little cloth.
    King.   Think we King Harry strong,
And, princes, look you strongly arm to meet him.
The kindred of him hath been flesh'd upon us, 50
And he is bred out of that bloody strain
That haunted us in our familiar paths.
Witness our too much memorable shame
When Cressy battle fatally was struck,
And all our princes captiv'd by the hand 55
Of that black name, Edward, Black Prince of Wales,
Whiles that his mountain sire, on mountain standing,

34 **exception** disagreement. 35 **constant** firm. 36 **forespent** former.
37 **Brutus** N. 39 **ordure** manure. 45 **proportions** . . . **fill'd** numbers necessary for defense are completed. 46 **of a weak** . . . **projection** if they are estimated on too small a scale. 50 **flesh'd**
aroused by the first taste of blood, or initiated in fighting (against
us). 54 **Cressy battle** the victory of Edward III over the French
at Crécy in 1346 N. **struck** fought. 57 **mountain sire** mighty sire
(or born among the mountains), Edward III.

Up in the air, crown'd with the golden sun,
Saw his heroical seed, and smil'd to see him
Mangle the work of nature and deface   60
The patterns that by God and by French fathers
Had twenty years been made. This is a stem
Of that victorious stock, and let us fear
The native mightiness and fate of him.

Enter a Messenger.

Messenger. Ambassadors from Harry King of Eng-
land   65
Do crave admittance to your majesty.
  King. We'll give them present audience. Go, and
bring them.
          [*Exeunt Messenger and certain Lords.*]
You see this chase is hotly follow'd, friends.
  Dolphin. Turn head and stop pursuit. For coward
dogs
Most spend their mouths when what they seem to
threaten   70
Runs far before them. Good my sovereign,
Take up the English short, and let them know
Of what a monarchy you are the head.
Self-love, my liege, is not so vile a sin
As self-neglecting.

Enter [Lords, with] Exeter [and train].

  King.   From our brother of England?
  Exeter. From him, and thus he greets your maj-
esty: 76
He wills you, in the name of God Almighty,

64 native . . . fate powerful inherited destiny. 67 present immediate. 69 Turn head stand at bay (from hunting). 70 spend
their mouths bark. 72 Take up . . . short answer curtly.
  40

That you divest yourself and lay apart
The borrow'd glories that by gift of heaven,
By law of nature and of nations, 'longs   80
To him and to his heirs—namely, the crown
And all wide-stretched honors that pertain
By custom and the ordinance of times
Unto the crown of France. That you may know
'Tis no sinister nor no awkward claim,   85
Pick'd from the wormholes of long-vanish'd days,
Nor from the dust of old oblivion rak'd,
He sends you this most memorable line,
In every branch truly demonstrative,
Willing you overlook this pedigree.   90
And when you find him evenly deriv'd
From his most fam'd of famous ancestors,
Edward the Third, he bids you then resign
Your crown and kingdom, indirectly held
From him, the native and true challenger.   95
    King. Or else what follows?
    Exeter. Bloody constraint, for if you hide the
        crown
Even in your hearts, there will he rake for it.
Therefore in fierce tempest is he coming,
In thunder and in earthquake, like a Jove,   100
That, if requiring fail, he will compel.
And bids you, in the bowels of the Lord,

---

83 **ordinance of times** usage of past ages. 85 **sinister** irregular;
stressed — ́ —. **awkward** indirect, perverse. 88 **memorable
line** noteworthy pedigree. 89 **demonstrative** proving his claims.
90 **overlook** look over. 91 **evenly** directly. 94 **indirectly** not in a
direct line of descent. 95 **challenger** claimant. 97 **constraint** force.
98 **Even** here and in l. 138 read 'e'en.' 99 **fierce** N. 101 **That** so
that. **requiring** requesting. 102 **in the bowels** 'by the mercy,' a
phrase from Holinshed (after Philippians 1:8).

Deliver up the crown, and to take mercy
On the poor souls for whom this hungry war
Opens his vasty jaws, and on your head   105
Turning the widows' tears, the orphans' cries,
The dead men's blood, the pining maidens' groans,
For husbands, fathers, and betrothed lovers
That shall be swallow'd in this controversy.   109
This is his claim, his threat'ning, and my message,
Unless the Dolphin be in presence here,
To whom expressly I bring greeting too.
  King. For us, we will consider of this further.
Tomorrow shall you bear our full intent   114
Back to our brother of England.
  Dolphin.   For the Dolphin,
I stand here for him. What to him from England?
  Exeter. Scorn and defiance, slight regard, con-
    tempt,
And anything that may not misbecome
The mighty sender, doth he prize you at.   119
Thus says my king. An if your father's highness
Do not, in grant of all demands at large,
Sweeten the bitter mock you sent his majesty,
He'll call you to so hot an answer of it
That caves and womby vaultages of France
Shall chide your trespass and return your mock   125
In second accent of his ordinance.
  Dolphin. Say, if my father render fair return,
It is against my will, for I desire
Nothing but odds with England. To that end,
As matching to his youth and vanity,   130

105 **vasty** vast. 107 **pining** Q; F *priuy.* 113 **For us** for my part.
121 **at large** in full. 124 **vaultages** caverns. 126 **second accent**
echo. **ordinance** ordnance, cannon. 129 **odds** quarrel. 130 **vanity**
frivolity.

I did present him with the Paris balls.

Exeter. He'll make your Paris Louvre shake for it,
Were it the mistress court of mighty Europe.
And be assur'd you'll find a difference,
As we his subjects have in wonder found,   135
Between the promise of his greener days
And these he masters now. Now he weighs time
Even to the utmost grain. That you shall read
In your own losses, if he stay in France.   139

King. Tomorrow shall you know our mind at full.
                              Flourish.

Exeter. Dispatch us with all speed, lest that our
    king
Come here himself to question our delay,
For he is footed in this land already.

King. You shall be soon dispatch'd with fair condi-
    tions.
A night is but small breath and little pause   145
To answer matters of this consequence.   *Exeunt.*

131 **Paris balls** the old term for tennis balls. 132 **Louvre** royal
palace in Paris N. 133 **mistress court** principal court (also a
tennis term). 136 **greener** younger, rawer. 137 **weighs time** i.e.
no longer wastes it N. 140 **Flourish** N. 143 **is footed** has a foot-
hold. 145 **breath** breathing space.

Act III

Flourish. Enter Chorus.

Thus with imagin'd wing our swift scene flies
In motion of no less celerity
Than that of thought. Suppose that you have seen
The well-appointed king at Hampton pier
Embark his royalty, and his brave fleet   5
With silken streamers the young Phoebus fanning.
Play with your fancies, and in them behold
Upon the hempen tackle ship boys climbing.
Hear the shrill whistle which doth order give
To sounds confus'd. Behold the threaden sails,   10
Borne with th' invisible and creeping wind,
Draw the huge bottoms through the furrow'd sea,
Breasting the lofty surge. O, do but think
You stand upon the rivage and behold
A city on th' inconstant billows dancing,   15
For so appears this fleet majestical,
Holding due course to Harflew. Follow, follow!
Grapple your minds to sternage of this navy,
And leave your England as dead midnight still,
Guarded with grandsires, babies, and old women, 20
Either past or not arriv'd to pith and puissance.

SD **Flourish** see II.Pro.SD N. 1 **imagin'd wing** the wing of
imagination. 3 **Than . . . Suppose** F ends l. 2 with *thought*.
4 **well-appointed** well-equipped. **Hampton** F *Douer*. 5 **brave** fine.
6 **Phoebus** the sun. **fanning** F *fayning*. 10 **threaden** linen. 14
rivage shore. 17 **Harflew** Harfleur, across from Le Havre at the
mouth of the Seine. 18 **sternage** the sterns. 21 **pith** strength.

For who is he whose chin is but enrich'd
With one appearing hair that will not follow
These cull'd and choice-drawn cavaliers to France?
Work, work your thoughts, and therein see a siege.
Behold the ordinance on their carriages,   26
With fatal mouths gaping on girded Harflew.
Suppose th' ambassador from the French comes
        back,
Tells Harry that the king doth offer him   29
Katharine his daughter, and with her, to dowry,
Some petty and unprofitable dukedoms.
The offer likes not. And the nimble gunner
With linstock now the divelish cannon touches,
                    Alarum, and chambers go off.
And down goes all before them. Still be kind,   34
And eche out our performance with your mind. *Exit.*

SCENE 1

*Alarum. Enter the King, Exeter, Bedford, and
Gloucester [and Soldiers, with] scaling ladders at
                    Harflew.*

King. Once more unto the breach, dear friends,
        once more,
Or close the wall up with our English dead.
In peace there's nothing so becomes a man
As modest stillness and humility.
But when the blast of war blows in our ears,   5

24 **choice-drawn** selected. 26 **ordinance** ordnance. 27 **girded** sur-
rounded, besieged. 32 **likes** pleases. 33 **linstock** combustibles at
the end of a staff for setting off cannon. SD **Alarum** trumpet call
to arms. **chambers** small cannon. 35 **eche out** eke out, supplement.

45

Then imitate the action of the tiger.
Stiffen the sinews, summon up the blood,
Disguise fair nature with hard-favor'd rage.
Then lend the eye a terrible aspect;
Let it pry through the portage of the head   10
Like the brass cannon. Let the brow o'erwhelm it
As fearfully as doth a galled rock
O'erhang and jutty his confounded base,
Swill'd with the wild and wasteful ocean.
Now set the teeth and stretch the nostril wide,   15
Hold hard the breath and bend up every spirit
To his full height. On, on, you noblest English,
Whose blood is fet from fathers of war proof!
Fathers that like so many Alexanders
Have in these parts from morn till even fought   20
And sheath'd their swords for lack of argument.
Dishonor not your mothers. Now attest
That those whom you call'd fathers did beget you.
Be copy now to men of grosser blood   24
And teach them how to war. And you, good yeomen,
Whose limbs were made in England, show us here
The mettle of your pasture. Let us swear
That you are worth your breeding, which I doubt
        not,
For there is none of you so mean and base
That hath not noble luster in your eyes.   30

---

7 summon F *commune* N. 8 **hard-favor'd** grim-faced. 9 **aspect**
stressed — ‿́. 10 **portage** portholes. 12 **galled** worn (by the sea).
13 **jutty** jut over. **confounded** worn, ruined. 14 **Swill'd with**
greedily swallowed by. **ocean** here trisyllabic. 18 **fet** fetched.
of war proof proved in war. 21 **argument** matter for dispute,
opposition. 24 **men** F *me*. 25 **yeomen** N. 27 **mettle . . . pasture**
the quality of your breeding N.

I see you stand like greyhounds in the slips,
Straining upon the start. The game's afoot!
Follow your spirit, and upon this charge
Cry 'God for Harry, England, and St. George!'
    [Exeunt.] Alarum, and chambers go off.

SCENE 2

Enter Nym, Bardolph, Pistol, and Boy.

Bardolph. On, on, on, on, on! to the breach, to the
breach!
Nym. Pray thee, corporal, stay. The knocks are too
hot, and, for mine own part, I have not a case of
lives. The humor of it is too hot, that is the very
plain song of it.   6
Pistol. The plain song is most just, for humors do
abound:

  Knocks go and come, God's vassals drop and die,
      And sword and shield   10
       In bloody field
     Doth win immortal fame.

Boy. Would I were in an alehouse in London! I
would give all my fame for a pot of ale and safety.
Pistol. And I: 15

31 **slips** leashes; collar, quickly released. 32 **Straining** F *Straying.*
34 **St. George** patron saint of England. 4 **case** set. 6 **plain song**
simple truth (simple melody without variations). 7 **just** correct.
9–12 **Knocks . . . fame** N.

> *If wishes would prevail with me,*
> *My purpose should not fail with me,*
> *But thither would I hie.*

Boy.   *As duly,*
>   *But not as truly,*   20
>   *As bird doth sing on bough.*

Enter Fluellen.

Fluellen. Up to the breach, you dogs! Avaunt, you cullions!   [*Driving them forward.*]

Pistol. Be merciful, great duke, to men of mold.
Abate thy rage, abate thy manly rage,   25
Abate thy rage, great duke!
Good bawcock, bate thy rage! Use lenity, sweet
chuck!

Nym. These be good humors! Your honor wins bad
humors.   *Exeunt [all but Boy].*

Boy. As young as I am, I have observ'd these three swashers. I am boy to them all three, but all they three, though they would serve me, could not be man to me; for indeed three such antics do not amount to a man. For Bardolph, he is white-liver'd and red-fac'd, by the means whereof a' faces it out, but fights not. For Pistol, he hath a killing tongue and a quiet sword, by the means whereof a' breaks words and keeps whole weapons. For Nym, he hath heard that men of few words are the best men, and therefore he scorns to say his prayers, lest a' should be thought

19 **duly** surely. 20 **truly** 'in tune' and 'faithfully.' 23 **cullions** rascals N. 24 **men of mold** men of earth, mortal men. 27 **bawcock** fine fellow (French *beau coq*). **chuck** chick. 31 **swashers** swaggerers. 32 **man** 'man' and 'servant.' 33 **antics** buffoons; F *Antiques.* 34 **For** as for. **white-liver'd** cowardly. 35 **faces it out** puts a good face on it. 37 **breaks words** 'mistakes his words' and 'breaks promises.' 39 **best** bravest.

a coward. But his few bad words are match'd with as few good deeds, for a' never broke any man's head but his own, and that was against a post when he was drunk. They will steal anything, and call it purchase. Bardolph stole a lute case, bore it twelve leagues, and sold it for three halfpence. Nym and Bardolph are sworn brothers in filching, and in Callice they stole a fire shovel. I knew by that piece of service the men would carry coals. They would have me as familiar with men's pockets as their gloves or their handkerchers, which makes much against my manhood, if I should take from another's pocket to put into mine; for it is plain pocketing up of wrongs. I must leave them and seek some better service. Their villainy goes against my weak stomach, and therefore I must cast it up.   *Exit.*

Enter Gower [and Fluellen.]

Gower. Captain Fluellen, you must come presently to the mines. The Duke of Gloucester would speak with you.   59
Fluellen. To the mines? Tell you the duke, it is not so good to come to the mines. For look you, the mines is not according to the disciplines of the war; the concavities of it is not sufficient. For look you, th' athversary, you may discuss unto the duke, look you, is digt himself four yard under the countermines.

42 **broke** bruised, drew blood from. 44–5 **purchase** booty. 47–8 **Callice** Calais; stressed —́ —. 48–9 **piece of service** warlike deed. 49 **carry coals** put up with insults; do the dirty work. 51 **makes** goes. 53 **pocketing . . . wrongs** pun ('stealing' and 'bearing insults'). 56 **cast it up** pun (throw it up). 57 **presently** immediately. 58 **mines** i.e. under the enemy's walls. **Gloucester** N. 62 **disciplines . . . war** military science.

By Cheshu, I think a' will plow up all, if there is not
better directions.   67

Gower. The Duke of Gloucester, to whom the order
of the siege is given, is altogether directed by an
Irishman, a very valiant gentleman, i' faith.

Fluellen. It is Captain Macmorris, is it not?   71

Gower. I think it be.

Fluellen. By Cheshu, he is an ass, as in the world!
I will verify as much in his beard. He has no more
directions in the true disciplines of the wars, look
you, of the Roman disciplines, than is a puppy dog.

Enter Macmorris and Captain Jamy.

Gower. Here a' comes, and the Scots captain, Captain Jamy, with him.   78

Fluellen. Captain Jamy is a marvelous falorous
gentleman, that is certain, and of great expedition
and knowledge in th' aunchiant wars, upon my particular knowledge of his directions. By Cheshu, he
will maintain his argument as well as any military
man in the world, in the disciplines of the pristine
wars of the Romans.   85

Jamy. I say gud day, Captain Fluellen.

Fluellen. God-den to your worship, good Captain
James.

Gower. How now, Captain Macmorris! Have you
quit the mines? Have the pioners given o'er?   90

Macmorris. By Chrish, la, tish ill done! The work
ish give over, the trompet sound the retreat. By my

66 **Cheshu** Jesu. 67 **directions** 'management,' or 'instructions to
his troops.' 71 **Fluellen** N. 74 **in . . . beard** to his face. 79
falorous valorous. 80 **expedition** readiness in argument. 81
aunchiant ancient. 86 **Jamy** N. 87 **God-den** good evening (commonly used in the afternoon). 90 **pioners** engineering troops,
sappers. **given o'er** given up.

hand, I swear, and my father's soul, the work ish ill
done! It ish give over. I would have blowed up the
town, so Chrish save me, la! in an hour. O, tish ill
done, tish ill done! By my hand, tish ill done!   96

Fluellen. Captain Macmorris, I beseech you now,
will you voutsafe me, look you, a few disputations
with you, as partly touching or concerning the disciplines of the war, the Roman wars, in the way of
argument, look you, and friendly communication—
partly to satisfy my opinion and partly for the satisfaction, look you, of my mind, as touching the
direction of the military discipline. That is the point.

Jamy. It sall be vary gud, gud feith, gud captens
bath, and I sall quit you with gud leve, as I may
pick occasion. That sall I, mary.   107

Macmorris. It is no time to discourse, so Chrish
save me! The day is hot, and the weather, and the
wars, and the king, and the dukes. It is no time to
discourse. The town is beseech'd, and the trompet
call us to the breach, and we talk, and, be Chrish, do
nothing! 'Tis shame for us all. So God sa' me, 'tis
shame to stand still, it is shame, by my hand! And
there is throats to be cut, and works to be done, and
there ish nothing done, so Chrish sa' me, la!   116

Jamy. By the mess, ere theise eyes of mine take
themselves to slomber, ay'll de gud service, or I'll lig
i' th' grund for it. Ay, or go to death! And I'll pay't
as valorously as I may, that sall I suerly do, that is
the breff and the long. Mary, I wad full fain heard
some question 'tween you tway.   122

Fluellen. Captain Macmorris, I think, look you,

---

106 **bath** both. **quit . . . leve** answer you with your permission.
111 **beseech'd** besieged. 117 **mess** Mass. **theise** these. 118 **de** do.
lig lie. 122 **tway** two.

under your correction, there is not many of your
nation—   125

Macmorris. Of my nation! What ish my nation? Ish
a villain, and a bastard, and a knave, and a rascal.
What ish my nation? Who talks of my nation?

Fluellen. Look you, if you take the matter otherwise than is meant, Captain Macmorris, peradventure I shall think you do not use me with that affa-
bility as in discretion you ought to use me, look you,
being as good a man as yourself, both in the disciplines of war, and in the derivation of my birth, and
in other particularities.   135

Macmorris. I do not know you so good a man as
myself. So Chrish save me, I will cut off your head!

Gower. Gentlemen both, you will mistake each other.

Jamy. Ah, that's a foul fault! *A parley [sounded].*

Gower. The town sounds a parley.   140

Fluellen. Captain Macmorris, when there is more
better opportunity to be required, look you, I will
be so bold as to tell you I know the disciplines of war.
And there is an end.   *Exeunt.*

SCENE 3

[Enter the Governor and some Citizens on the walls.]
Enter the King [Henry] and all his train before the
gates.

King. How yet resolves the governor of the town?

124 under . . . correction correct me if I'm wrong. 139 parley
trumpet summons to a parley. 142 required probably 'found.'
SD gates the gates of Harfleur; in F the Governor enters at l. 43.

This is the latest parle we will admit.
Therefore to our best mercy give yourselves,
Or like to men proud of destruction
Defy us to our worst. For, as I am a soldier,   5
A name that in my thoughts becomes me best,
If I begin the batt'ry once again,
I will not leave the half-achiev'd Harflew
Till in her ashes she lie buried.
The gates of mercy shall be all shut up,   10
And the flesh'd soldier, rough and hard of heart,
In liberty of bloody hand shall range
With conscience wide as hell, mowing like grass
Your fresh fair virgins and your flow'ring infants.
What is it then to me if impious War,   15
Array'd in flames like to the prince of fiends,
Do with his smirch'd complexion all fell feats
Enlink'd to waste and desolation?
What is't to me, when you yourselves are cause,
If your pure maidens fall into the hand   20
Of hot and forcing violation?
What rein can hold licentious wickedness
When down the hill he holds his fierce career?
We may as bootless spend our vain command
Upon th' enraged soldiers in their spoil   25
As send precepts to the leviathan
To come ashore. Therefore, you men of Harflew,
Take pity of your town and of your people
Whiles yet my soldiers are in my command,

2 latest parle last parley N. 4 proud of destruction proudly headed
toward self-destruction. 8 half-achiev'd half won. Harflew Harfleur. 11 flesh'd made fierce by the taste of blood. 12 liberty
license. 17 fell cruel. 18 Enlink'd to associated with. 23 career
swift course. 24 bootless vainly. 26 precepts summons (a legal
term); stressed — ´. leviathan whale. 27 ashore F ends l. 26
here.

Whiles yet the cool and temperate wind of grace   30
O'erblows the filthy and contagious clouds
Of heady murther, spoil, and villainy.
If not—why, in a moment look to see
The blind and bloody soldier with foul hand   34
Defile the locks of your shrill-shrieking daughters,
Your fathers taken by the silver beards
And their most reverend heads dash'd to the walls,
Your naked infants spitted upon pikes
Whiles the mad mothers with their howls confus'd
Do break the clouds, as did the wives of Jewry   40
At Herod's bloody-hunting slaughtermen.
What say you? Will you yield, and this avoid,
Or, guilty in defense, be thus destroy'd?

  Governor. Our expectation hath this day an end.
The Dolphin, whom of succors we entreated,   45
Returns us that his pow'rs are yet not ready
To raise so great a siege. Therefore, great king,
We yield our town and lives to thy soft mercy.
Enter our gates, dispose of us and ours,
For we no longer are defensible.   50

  King. Open your gates. Come, Uncle Exeter,
Go you and enter Harflew. There remain,
And fortify it strongly 'gainst the French.
Use mercy to them all. For us, dear uncle,
The winter coming on, and sickness growing   55
Upon our soldiers, we will retire to Callice.
Tonight in Harflew will we be your guest;

30 **temperate** read 'temp'rate.' **grace** mercy. 31 **O'erblows** blows away. **contagious** clouds and mists were thought to carry contagion. 32 **heady** headstrong, violent; F *headly.* 35 **Defile** F *Desire.* 40 **break** pierce. 41 **slaughtermen** i.e. the Slaughter of the Innocents (see Matthew 2:16–18). 44 **expectation** hope. 45 **of** for. 50 **defensible** capable of defending ourselves. 54 **all. For us** F *all for vs.* 56 **Callice** Calais.

Tomorrow for the march are we address'd.

Flourish, and enter the town.

SCENE 4

Enter Katharine and [Alice,] an old gentlewoman.

Katharine. Alice, tu as été en Angleterre, et tu parles bien le langage.

Alice. Un peu, madame.

Katharine. Je te prie, m'enseignez. Il faut que j'apprenne à parler. Comment appelez-vous la main en anglais?   6

Alice. La main? Elle est appelée de hand.

Katharine. De hand. Et les doigts?

Alice. Les doigts? Ma foi, j'oublie les doigts, mais je me souviendrai. Les doigts? Je pense qu'ils sont appelés de fingres—oui, de fingres.   11

Katharine. La main, de hand; les doigts, de fingres.

58 address'd prepared. 3 Un peu see Appendix A N. 8 Et les doigts N.

Translation.

Katharine. Alice, you have been in England and speak the language well.

Alice. A little, my lady.

Katharine. I pray you, teach me. I must learn to speak it. What do you call la main in English?

Alice. La main? It is called de hand.

Katharine. De hand. And les doigts?

Alice. Les doigts? Dear me, I forget les doigts, but I shall remember. Les doigts? I think that they are called de fingres—yes, de fingres.

Katharine. La main, de hand; les doigts, de fingres. I think that I

Je pense que je suis le bon écolier. J'ai gagné deux mots d'anglais vitement. Comment appelez-vous les ongles?   15

Alice. Les ongles? Nous les appelons de nayles.

Katharine. De nayles. Écoutez. Dites-moi si je parle bien: de hand, de fingres, et de nayles.

Alice. C'est bien dit, madame; il est fort bon anglais.   20

Katharine. Dites-moi l'anglais pour le bras.

Alice. De arm, madame.

Katharine. Et le coude?

Alice. D' elbow.   24

Katharine. D' elbow. Je m'en fais la répétition de tous les mots que vous m'avez appris dès à présent.

Alice. Il est trop difficile, madame, comme je pense.

Katharine. Excusez-moi, Alice. Écoutez: d' hand, de fingre, de nayles, d' arma, de bilbow.

Alice. D' elbow, madame.   30

am a good scholar. I have acquired two words of English quickly. What do you call les ongles?

Alice. Les ongles? We call them de nayles.

Katharine. De nayles. Listen. Tell me whether or not I speak correctly: de hand, de fingres, and de nayles.

Alice. That is correct, my lady; it is very good English.

Katharine. Tell me the English for le bras.

Alice. De arm, my lady.

Katharine. And le coude?

Alice. D' elbow.

Katharine. D' elbow. I am going to repeat all the words you have taught me up to now.

Alice. It is too difficult, my lady, I think.

Katharine. Pardon me, Alice. Listen: d' hand, de fingre, de nayles, d' arma, de bilbow.

Alice. D' elbow, my lady.

Katharine. O, Seigneur Dieu, je m'en oublie! D' elbow. Comment appelez-vous le col?

Alice. De nick, madame.

Katharine. De nick. Et le menton?

Alice. De chin. 35

Katharine. De sin. Le col, de nick; le menton, de sin.

Alice. Oui. Sauf votre honneur, en vérité, vous prononcez les mots aussi droit que les natifs d'Angleterre. 39

Katharine. Je ne doute point d'apprendre, par la grâce de Dieu, et en peu de temps.

Alice. N'avez-vous pas déjà oublié ce que je vous ai enseigné?

Katharine. Non, je réciterai à vous promptement: d' hand, de fingre, de maylees— 45

Alice. De nayles, madame.

Katharine. De nayles, de arm, de ilbow.

Alice. Sauf votre honneur, d' elbow.

Katharine. O, Lord, I forget! D' elbow. What do you call le col?

Alice. De nick, my lady.

Katharine. De nick. And le menton?

Alice. De chin.

Katharine. De sin. Le col, de nick; le menton, de sin.

Alice. Yes. Saving your grace, in truth you pronounce the words as well as the people of England [do].

Katharine. I don't doubt that I shall learn, with God's help, and in a short time.

Alice. Haven't you already forgotten what I have taught you?

Katharine. No, I shall recite to you at once: d' hand, de fingre, de maylees—

Alice. De nayles, my lady.

Katharine. De nayles, de arm, de ilbow.

Alice. Saving your grace, d' elbow.

Katharine. Ainsi dis-je: d' elbow, de nick, et de sin.
Comment appelez-vous le pied et la robe?   50

Alice. Le foot, madame, et le count.

Katharine. Le foot et le count! O, Seigneur Dieu!
ils sont les mots de son mauvais, corruptible, gros, et
impudique, et non pour les dames d'honneur d'user.
Je ne voudrais prononcer ces mots devant les seigneurs de France pour tout le monde. Foh! Le foot
et le count! Néanmoins, je réciterai une autre fois
ma leçon ensemble: d' hand, de fingre, de nayles, d'arm,
d' elbow, de nick, de sin, de foot, le count.

Alice. Excellent, madame!   60

Katharine. C'est assez pour une fois. Allons-nous
à dîner.   *Exeunt.*

Katharine. That's what I said: d' elbow, de nick, and de sin.
What do you call le pied and la robe?

Alice. Le foot, my lady, and le count.

Katharine. Le foot and le count! O, Lord! those are naughty
words, wicked, coarse, and immodest and [are] not for fine ladies
to use. I wouldn't pronounce these words before the lords of
France for the whole world. Fie! le foot and le count! Nevertheless, I shall recite my whole lesson once more: d' hand, de fingre,
de nayles, d' arm, d' elbow, de nick, de sin, de foot, le count.

Alice. Excellent, my lady.

Katharine. That's enough for one time. Let's go to dinner.

SCENE 5

Enter the King of France, the Dolphin, [the Duke of Britaine,] the Constable of France, and others.

King. 'Tis certain he hath pass'd the river Somme.
Constable. And if he be not fought withal, my lord,
Let us not live in France. Let us quit all
And give our vineyards to a barbarous people.   4
Dolphin. O, Dieu vivant! Shall a few sprays of us,
The emptying of our fathers' luxury,
Our scions, put in wild and savage stock,
Spurt up so suddenly into the clouds
And overlook their grafters?
Britaine. Normans, but bastard Normans, Norman
  bastards!   10
Mort Dieu! ma vie! if they march along
Unfought withal, but I will sell my dukedom
To buy a slobb'ry and a dirty farm
In that nook-shotten isle of Albion.
Constable. Dieu de batailles! Where have they this
  mettle?   15
Is not their climate foggy, raw, and dull,
On whom, as in despite, the sun looks pale,
Killing their fruit with frowns? Can sodden water,
A drench for sur-rein'd jades, their barley broth,

SD **Britaine** N. 2 **withal** with. 5 **sprays** offshoots. 6 **luxury** lust.
9 **overlook . . . grafters** N. 11 **Mort . . . vie** F *Mort du ma vie*
and most editors read *Mort de ma vie.* 13 **slobb'ry** muddy. 14
nook-shotten running out into corners or angles. 15 **batailles**
trisyllabic. **Where** whence. **mettle** stuff, courage. 17 **despite** spite.
18 **sodden** boiled. 19 **drench** medicinal draught. **sur-rein'd** over-
ridden. **jades** horses (contemptuous).

Decoct their cold blood to such valiant heat? 20
And shall our quick blood, spirited with wine,
Seem frosty? O, for honor of our land,
Let us not hang like roping icicles
Upon our houses' thatch, whiles a more frosty people
Sweat drops of gallant youth in our rich fields ! 25
Poor we may call them in their native lords.
  Dolphin. By faith and honor,
Our madams mock at us and plainly say
Our mettle is bred out, and they will give
Their bodies to the lust of English youth 30
To new-store France with bastard warriors.
  Britaine. They bid us to the English dancing
    schools
And teach lavoltas high and swift corantos,
Saying our grace is only in our heels
And that we are most lofty runaways. 35
  King. Where is Montjoy the herald? Speed him
    hence.
Let him greet England with our sharp defiance.
Up, princes, and, with spirit of honor edg'd
More sharper than your swords, hie to the field.
Charles Delabreth, High Constable of France, 40
You Dukes of Orleans, Bourbon, and of Berri,
Alençon, Brabant, Bar, and Burgundy,
Jaques Chatillon, Rambures, Vaudemont,
Beaumont, Grandpré, Roussi, and Faulconbridge,
Foix, Lestrake, Bouciqualt, and Charolois— 45

20 **Decoct** warm up. 23 **roping** hanging down like ropes. 26 **Poor**
. . . **lords** i.e. their fields have bred leaders of poor quality.
may F2; not in F. 33 **lavoltas** high jumping dances. **corantos**
rapid sliding dances. 36 **Montjoy** title of the chief herald or
king-at-arms of France. 38 **spirit** here and elsewhere read 'sprite'
or 'spir't.' 40–5 **Charles . . . Charolois** all these names are taken
from Holinshed. 44 **Faulconbridge** N.

High dukes, great princes, barons, lords, and
    knights,
For your great seats now quit you of great shames.
Bar Harry England, that sweeps through our land
With pennons painted in the blood of Harflew.
Rush on his host as doth the melted snow   50
Upon the valleys, whose low vassal seat
The Alps doth spit and void his rheum upon.
Go down upon him—you have power enough—
And in a captive chariot into Roan
Bring him our prisoner.
   Constable.   This becomes the great.   55
Sorry am I his numbers are so few,
His soldiers sick and famish'd in their march.
For I am sure, when he shall see our army,
He'll drop his heart into the sink of fear
And for achievement offer us his ransom.   60
   King. Therefore, Lord Constable, haste on Mont-
    joy,
And let him say to England that we send
To know what willing ransom he will give.
Prince Dolphin, you shall stay with us in Roan.
   Dolphin. Not so, I do beseech your majesty.   65
   King. Be patient, for you shall remain with us.
Now forth, Lord Constable and princes all,
And quickly bring us word of England's fall. *Exeunt.*

46 **knights** F *Kings.* 47 **seats** estates, fiefs. **quit you** absolve yourselves. 52 **void his rheum** spit. 54 **Roan** Rouen. 60 **for achievement** i.e. instead of victory.

SCENE 6

Enter Captains, English and Welsh: Gower and Fluellen.

Gower. How now, Captain Fluellen! Come you from the bridge?

Fluellen. I assure you there is very excellent services committed at the bridge.

Gower. Is the Duke of Exeter safe?　　　　　　5

Fluellen. The Duke of Exeter is as magnanimous as Agamemnon, and a man that I love and honor with my soul, and my heart, and my duty, and my live, and my living, and my uttermost power. He is not— God be praised and blessed!—any hurt in the world, but keeps the bridge most valiantly, with excellent discipline. There is an aunchient lieutenant there at the pridge, I think in my very conscience he is as valiant a man as Mark Antony, and he is a man of no estimation in the world, but I did see him do as gallant service.　　　　　　16

Gower. What do you call him?

Fluellen. He is call'd Aunchient Pistol.

Gower. I know him not.

Enter Pistol.

Fluellen. Here is the man.　　　　　　20

Pistol. Captain, I thee beseech to do me favors.

SD **English and Welsh** N. **7 Agamemnon** general of the Greek forces that besieged Troy. **8-9 live . . . living** N. **12 discipline** military science. **aunchient lieutenant** two ridiculously juxtaposed titles; perhaps 'sublieutenant.' **aunchient** ancient (ensign). **15 estimation** reputation. **21-2 Captain . . . well** F prints all of Pistol's speeches in this scene as prose.

62

The Duke of Exeter doth love thee well.

Fluellen. Ay, I praise God, and I have merited some
love at his hands.   24

Pistol. Bardolph, a soldier firm and sound of heart,
And of buxom valor, hath by cruel fate
And giddy Fortune's furious fickle wheel,
That goddess blind,
That stands upon the rolling restless stone—   29

Fluellen. By your patience, Aunchient Pistol. Fortune is painted blind, with a muffler afore his eyes,
to signify to you, that Fortune is blind. And she is
painted also with a wheel, to signify to you, which
is the moral of it, that she is turning and inconstant,
and mutability, and variation. And her foot, look
you, is fixed upon a spherical stone, which rolls, and
rolls, and rolls. In good truth, the poet makes a most
excellent description of it. Fortune is an excellent
moral.

Pistol. Fortune is Bardolph's foe, and frowns on
    him,   40
For he hath stol'n a pax, and hanged must a' be—
A damned death!
Let gallows gape for dog, let man go free,
And let not hemp his windpipe suffocate.
But Exeter hath given the doom of death   45
For pax of little price.
Therefore go speak—the duke will hear thy voice,
And let not Bardolph's vital thread be cut
With edge of penny cord and vile reproach.   49
Speak, captain, for his life, and I will thee requite.

Fluellen. Aunchient Pistol, I do partly understand
your meaning.

26 buxom lively. 27 furious cruel. 31 his F; often emended to *her.*
39 moral a symbolical figure. 41 pax N.

Pistol. Why, then, rejoice therefore.　　　　　　　53

Fluellen. Certainly, aunchient, it is not a thing to
rejoice at. For if, look you, he were my brother, I
would desire the duke to use his good pleasure and
put him to execution, for discipline ought to be used.

Pistol. Die and be damn'd! and figo for thy friendship!

Fluellen. It is well.　　　　　　　60

Pistol. The fig of Spain!　　　　　　*Exit.*

Fluellen. Very good.

Gower. Why, this is an arrant counterfeit rascal.
I remember him now—a bawd, a cutpurse.

Fluellen. I'll assure you, a' utt'red as prave words
at the pridge as you shall see in a summer's day. But
it is very well. What he has spoke to me, that is well,
I warrant you, when time is serve.　　　　　　　68

Gower. Why, 'tis a gull, a fool, a rogue, that now
and then goes to the wars to grace himself, at his
return into London, under the form of a soldier. And
such fellows are perfit in the great commanders'
names, and they will learn you by rote where services
were done—at such and such a sconce, at such a
breach, at such a convoy; who came off bravely, who
was shot, who disgrac'd, what terms the enemy stood
on. And this they con perfitly in the phrase of war,
which they trick up with new-tuned oaths. And what
a beard of the general's cut and a horrid suit of the
camp will do among foaming bottles and ale-wash'd
wits is wonderful to be thought on. But you must

58 figo N. 63 **arrant** out-and-out. 64 **bawd** pander. 65 **prave** brave,
i.e. fine. 68 **is serve** i.e. shall serve. 69 **gull** simpleton. 72 **perfit**
perfect. 73 **learn** teach. 74 **sconce** fortification. 76 **stood** insisted.
77 **con** learn by heart. 78 **new-tuned** newly composed.

learn to know such slanders of the age, or else you
may be marvelously mistook.   83

Fluellen. I tell you what, Captain Gower. I do per-
ceive he is not the man that he would gladly make
show to the world he is. If I find a hole in his coat,
I will tell him my mind. [*Drum within.*] Hark you,
the king is coming, and I must speak with him from
the pridge.

*Drum and colors. Enter the King [Henry] and his
poor Soldiers [and Gloucester].*

Fluellen. God pless your majesty!   90
King. How now, Fluellen! Cam'st thou from the
bridge?
Fluellen. Ay, so please your majesty. The Duke of
Exeter has very gallantly maintain'd the pridge. The
French is gone off, look you, and there is gallant and
most prave passages. Marry, th' athversary was
have possession of the pridge, but he is enforced to
retire, and the Duke of Exeter is master of the
pridge. I can tell your majesty, the duke is a prave
man.   100

King. What men have you lost, Fluellen?
Fluellen. The perdition of th' athversary hath been
very great, reasonable great. Marry, for my part, I
think the duke hath lost never a man but one that
is like to be executed for robbing a church—one Bardolph, if your majesty know the man. His face is all
bubukles and whelks, and knobs, and flames o' fire,
and his lips blows at his nose, and it is like a coal of

---

82 **slanders** scandals, abuses. 86 **hole . . . coat** i.e. some weak
spot in his record. 88 **from** about, or with news from. 96 **passages**
deeds. 102 **perdition** loss. 107 **bubukles** Fluellen's word for 'car-
buncles.' **whelks** boils.

fire, sometimes plue, and sometimes red; but his nose
is executed, and his fire's out.   110

King. We would have all such offenders so cut off.
And we give express charge that in our marches
through the country there be nothing compell'd from
the villages, nothing taken but paid for, none of the
French upbraided or abused in disdainful language.
For when lenity and cruelty play for a kingdom, the
gentler gamester is the soonest winner.   117

Tucket. Enter Montjoy.

Montjoy. You know me by my habit.

King. Well then, I know thee. What shall I know of
thee?

Montjoy. My master's mind.

King. Unfold it.   122

Montjoy. Thus says my king: Say thou to Harry
of England: Though we seem'd dead, we did but
sleep. Advantage is a better soldier than rashness.
Tell him we could have rebuk'd him at Harflew, but
that we thought not good to bruise an injury till it
were full ripe. Now we speak upon our cue, and our
voice is imperial. England shall repent his folly, see
his weakness, and admire our sufferance. Bid him
therefore consider of his ransom, which must proportion the losses we have borne, the subjects we have

113 **compell'd** forced. 116 **lenity** Q; F *Leuitie*. SD **Tucket** trumpet
signal. 118 **habit** i.e. his herald's tabard coat. 125 **Advantage**
caution, awaiting a favorable opportunity. 127 **bruise** squeeze
(as in squeezing a boil). 128 **upon . . . cue** at the right moment.
129 **England** i.e. Henry. 130 **admire . . . sufferance** wonder at
our forbearance. 131–2 **proportion** be in proportion to.

lost, the disgrace we have digested; which in weight
to reanswer, his pettiness would bow under. For our
losses, his exchequer is too poor. For th' effusion of
our blood, the muster of his kingdom too faint a
number. And for our disgrace, his own person kneel-
ing at our feet but a weak and worthless satisfaction.
To this add defiance, and tell him, for conclusion, he
hath betrayed his followers, whose condemnation is
pronounc'd. So far my king and master; so much
my office.   142

King. What is thy name? I know thy quality.

Montjoy. Montjoy.

King. Thou dost thy office fairly. Turn thee back,
And tell thy king I do not seek him now,
But could be willing to march on to Callice
Without impeachment. For, to say the sooth,
Though 'tis no wisdom to confess so much
Unto an enemy of craft and vantage,   150
My people are with sickness much enfeebl'd,
My numbers lessen'd, and those few I have
Almost no better than so many French;
Who when they were in health, I tell thee, herald,
I thought upon one pair of English legs   155
Did march three Frenchmen. Yet forgive me, God,
That I do brag thus! This your air of France
Hath blown that vice in me. I must repent.
Go therefore, tell thy master here I am.
My ransom is this frail and worthless trunk;   160
My army but a weak and sickly guard.

133-4 **in weight . . . under** i.e. his public resources would col-
lapse under any attempt to compensate fully. 143 **quality** pro-
fession. 145 **dost** F *doo'st;* see IV.7.162. **fairly** splendidly. 147
Callice Calais. 148 **impeachment** hindrance. 150 **of . . . vantage**
who is cunning and has the advantage. 158 **blown** puffed up.

Yet, God before, tell him we will come on,
Though France himself and such another neighbor
Stand in our way. There's for thy labor, Montjoy.
Go bid thy master well advise himself.   165
If we may pass, we will. If we be hind'red,
We shall your tawny ground with your red blood
Discolor. And so, Montjoy, fare you well.
The sum of all our answer is but this:
We would not seek a battle as we are,   170
Nor, as we are, we say we will not shun it.
So tell your master.

    Montjoy. I shall deliver so. Thanks to your high-
      ness.   *[Exit.]*

    Gloucester. I hope they will not come upon us now.
    King. We are in God's hand, brother, not in theirs.
March to the bridge. It now draws toward night.
Beyond the river we'll encamp ourselves,   177
And on tomorrow bid them march away.   *Exeunt.*

SCENE 7

*Enter the Constable of France, the Lord Rambures,
Orleans, Dolphin, with others.*

    Constable. Tut, I have the best armor of the world.
Would it were day!

    Orleans. You have an excellent armor, but let my
horse have his due.

    Constable. It is the best horse of Europe.   5

164 **There's . . . labor** he gives the herald a purse or some
valuable. **166–8 If we . . . Discolor** N. 167 **tawny** yellow.
SD **Dolphin** N.

Orleans. Will it never be morning?

Dolphin. My lord of Orleans, and my Lord High Constable, you talk of horse and armor?

Orleans. You are as well provided of both as any prince in the world.   10

Dolphin. What a long night is this! I will not change my horse with any that treads but on four pasterns. Ça, ha! he bounds from the earth as if his entrails were hairs: le cheval volant, the Pegasus, chez les narines de feu! When I bestride him, I soar, I am a hawk. He trots the air. The earth sings when he touches it. The basest horn of his hoof is more musical than the pipe of Hermes.

Orleans. He's of the color of the nutmeg.   19

Dolphin. And of the heat of the ginger. It is a beast for Perseus: he is pure air and fire, and the dull elements of earth and water never appear in him, but only in patient stillness while his rider mounts him. He is indeed a horse, and all other jades you may call beasts.   25

Constable. Indeed, my lord, it is a most absolute and excellent horse.

Dolphin. It is the prince of palfreys. His neigh is like the bidding of a monarch, and his countenance enforces homage.   30

Orleans. No more, cousin.

Dolphin. Nay, the man hath no wit that cannot

---

13 **pasterns** the part of a horse's leg between hoof and fetlock; F2; F *postures.* 13–4 **as if . . . hairs** i.e. as if he were stuffed with hair (like a tennis ball) N. 14–5 **le cheval . . . feu** Pegasus, the flying horse with nostrils of fire. 17 **basest horn** note pun. 18 **Hermes** who charmed Argus to sleep by playing on his pipe. 21 **Perseus** the Greek hero who rode on Pegasus. 24 **jades** N. 26 **absolute** perfect. 28 **palfreys** saddle horses, usually for ladies.

from the rising of the lark to the lodging of the lamb vary deserved praise on my palfrey. It is a theme as fluent as the sea. Turn the sands into eloquent tongues, and my horse is argument for them all. 'Tis a subject for a sovereign to reason on, and for a sovereign's sovereign to ride on, and for the world, familiar to us and unknown, to lay apart their particular functions and wonder at him. I once writ a sonnet in his praise, and began thus, 'Wonder of nature—'

Orleans. I have heard a sonnet begin so to one's mistress. 44

Dolphin. Then did they imitate that which I compos'd to my courser, for my horse is my mistress.

Orleans. Your mistress bears well.

Dolphin. Me well, which is the prescript praise and perfection of a good and particular mistress.

Constable. Nay, for methought yesterday your mistress shrewdly shook your back. 51

Dolphin. So perhaps did yours.

Constable. Mine was not bridled.

Dolphin. O, then belike she was old and gentle, and you rode like a kern of Ireland, your French hose off and in your strait strossers. 56

Constable. You have good judgment in horsemanship.

Dolphin. Be warn'd by me then. They that ride so, and ride not warily, fall into foul bogs. I had rather have my horse to my mistress. 61

Constable. I had as live have my mistress a jade.

33 **lodging** lying down. 36 **argument** subject. 37 **reason** discourse. 48 **prescript** prescribed. 49 **particular** belonging only to one lover. 51 **shrewdly** viciously. 55 **kern** Irish foot soldier. **French hose** baggy breeches. 56 **strait strossers** tight trousers, i.e. bare-legged or in underpants. 62 **live** lief.

Dolphin. I tell thee, Constable, my mistress wears his own hair.

Constable. I could make as true a boast as that if I had a sow to my mistress.   66

Dolphin. 'Le chien est retourné à son propre vomissement, et la truie lavée au bourbier.' Thou mak'st use of anything.

Constable. Yet do I not use my horse for my mistress, or any such proverb so little kin to the purpose.

Rambures. My Lord Constable, the armor that I saw in your tent tonight—are those stars or suns upon it?   75

Constable. Stars, my lord.

Dolphin. Some of them will fall tomorrow, I hope.

Constable. And yet my sky shall not want.

Dolphin. That may be, for you bear a many superfluously, and 'twere more honor some were away.

Constable. Ev'n as your horse bears your praises, who would trot as well were some of your brags dismounted.   83

Dolphin. Would I were able to load him with his desert! Will it never be day? I will trot tomorrow a mile, and my way shall be paved with English faces.

Constable. I will not say so for fear I should be fac'd out of my way. But I would it were morning, for I would fain be about the ears of the English.

Rambures. Who will go to hazard with me for twenty prisoners?   91

Constable. You must first go yourself to hazard ere you have them.

Dolphin. 'Tis midnight. I'll go arm myself.   *Exit*.

66 to as. 67–8 Le . . . bourbier N. 68–9 Thou . . . anything i.e. to win an argument. 88 fac'd . . . way outfaced, put to shame; driven off. 90 go to hazard play craps.

Orleans. The Dolphin longs for morning.   95

Rambures. He longs to eat the English.

Constable. I think he will eat all he kills.

Orleans. By the white hand of my lady, he's a gallant prince.

Constable. Swear by her foot, that she may tread out the oath.   101

Orleans. He is simply the most active gentleman of France.

Constable. Doing is activity, and he will still be doing.   105

Orleans. He never did harm that I heard of.

Constable. Nor will do none tomorrow. He will keep that good name still.

Orleans. I know him to be valiant.

Constable. I was told that by one that knows him better than you.   111

Orleans. What's he?

Constable. Marry, he told me so himself, and he said he car'd not who knew it.

Orleans. He needs not. It is no hidden virtue in him.

Constable. By my faith, sir, but it is. Never anybody saw it but his lackey. 'Tis a hooded valor, and when it appears it will bate.

Orleans. 'Ill will never said well.'   119

Constable. I will cap that proverb with 'There is flattery in friendship.'

Orleans. And I will take up that with 'Give the devil his due.'

100–1 **tread out** treat with contempt. 104 **still** always. 117 **lackey** a running footman, servant (the only person he has stood up to). 117–18 **hooded . . . bate** N. 119–28 **Ill will . . . shot** in this game of 'capping proverbs' the one who has the last word wins.

Constable. Well plac'd. There stands your friend
for the devil. Have at the very eye of that proverb
with 'A pox of the devil!' 126

Orleans. You are the better at proverbs, by how
much 'A fool's bolt is soon shot.'

Constable. You have shot over.

Orleans. 'Tis not the first time you were overshot.

Enter a Messenger.

Messenger. My Lord High Constable, the English
lie within fifteen hundred paces of your tents. 132

Constable. Who hath measur'd the ground?

Messenger. The Lord Grandpré.

Constable. A valiant and most expert gentleman.
Would it were day! Alas, poor Harry of England!
He longs not for the dawning as we do.

Orleans. What a wretched and peevish fellow is this
King of England, to mope with his fat-brain'd followers so far out of his knowledge! 140

Constable. If the English had any apprehension,
they would run away.

Orleans. That they lack, for if their heads had any
intellectual armor, they could never wear such heavy
headpieces. 145

Rambures. That island of England breeds very valiant creatures. Their mastiffs are of unmatchable
courage.

127–8 **how much** as much as. 128 **bolt** arrow. 129 **shot over** missed
the target. 130 **overshot** outshot. 138 **peevish** foolish. 139 **fat-
brain'd** fat-headed. 140 **out . . . knowledge** beyond his experience or understanding. 141 **apprehension** common sense (pun on
'fear'). 147 **mastiffs** well known throughout Europe for their
bull- and bear-baiting.

Orleans. Foolish curs, that run winking into the mouth of a Russian bear and have their heads crush'd like rotten apples! You may as well say that's a valiant flea that dare eat his breakfast on the lip of a lion.   153

Constable. Just, just. And the men do sympathize with the mastiffs in robustious and rough coming on, leaving their wits with their wives. And then give them great meals of beef and iron and steel, they will eat like wolves and fight like devils.

Orleans. Ay, but these English are shrowdly out of beef.   160

Constable. Then shall we find tomorrow they have only stomachs to eat and none to fight. Now is it time to arm. Come, shall we about it?

Orleans. It is now two o'clock. But let me see, by ten

We shall have each a hundred Englishmen. *Exeunt.*

149 **winking** with their eyes shut. 150 **Russian bear** highly prized in bear-baiting. 154 **Just, just** exactly so. 154–5 **sympathize with** resemble. 155 **robustious** violent. **coming on** attack. 156–8 **give . . . devils** N. 159 **shrowdly** shrewdly, grievously. 162 **stomachs** inclinations.

Act IV

[Enter] Chorus.

Now entertain conjecture of a time
When creeping murmur and the poring dark
Fills the wide vessel of the universe.
From camp to camp through the foul womb of night
The hum of either army stilly sounds,   5
That the fix'd sentinels almost receive
The secret whispers of each other's watch.
Fire answers fire, and through their paly flames
Each battle sees the other's umber'd face.   9
Steed threatens steed, in high and boastful neighs
Piercing the night's dull ear. And from the tents
The armorers, accomplishing the knights,
With busy hammers closing rivets up,
Give dreadful note of preparation.
The country cocks do crow, the clocks do toll,   15
And the third hour of drowsy morning name.
Proud of their numbers and secure in soul,
The confident and overlusty French
Do the low-rated English play at dice,
And chide the creeple tardy-gaited night   20
Who like a foul and ugly witch doth limp
So tediously away. The poor condemned English,

1 **entertain conjecture** imagine. 2 **poring** eye-straining. 5 **stilly** quietly. 6 **That** so that. 8 **paly** pale. 9 **battle** army. **umber'd** dark brown, i.e. shadowy. 12 **accomplishing** completing the equipment of. 13 **rivets** N. 16 **name** F *nam'd*. 17 **secure** carefree, overconfident. 18 **overlusty** too merry. 19 **play at dice** i.e. play for their lives. 20 **creeple** cripple.

Like sacrifices, by their watchful fires
Sit patiently and inly ruminate
The morning's danger. And their gesture sad,   25
Investing lank-lean cheeks and war-worn coats,
Presenteth them unto the gazing moon
So many horrid ghosts. O, now, who will behold
The royal captain of this ruin'd band   29
Walking from watch to watch, from tent to tent,
Let him cry 'Praise and glory on his head!'
For forth he goes and visits all his host,
Bids them good morrow with a modest smile,
And calls them brothers, friends, and countrymen.
Upon his royal face there is no note   35
How dread an army hath enrounded him,
Nor doth he dedicate one jot of color
Unto the weary and all-watched night,
But freshly looks and overbears attaint
With cheerful semblance and sweet majesty,   40
That every wretch, pining and pale before,
Beholding him, plucks comfort from his looks.
A largess universal like the sun
His liberal eye doth give to every one,
Thawing cold fear; that mean and gentle all   45
Behold, as may unworthiness define,
A little touch of Harry in the night.
And so our scene must to the battle fly,

24 inly inwardly. 25 gesture sad serious bearing. 26 **Investing** clothing with dignity. 27 Presenteth F *Presented*. 33 good morrow good morning. 35 note sign. 37 dedicate sacrifice. 38 all-watched sleepless throughout. 39 **overbears attaint** conquers any sign of fatigue and fear. 40 **semblance** appearance. 41 **That** so that. 43 **like the sun** N. 45 **mean and gentle** those of low birth and gentlemen. 46 **as . . . define** so far as our poor abilities can depict it. 47 **touch** glimpse.

Where—O, for pity!—we shall much disgrace
With four or five most vile and ragged foils,   50
Right ill-dispos'd in brawl ridiculous,
The name of Agincourt. Yet sit and see,
Minding true things by what their mock'ries be. *Exit.*

SCENE 1

Enter the King [Henry], Bedford, and Gloucester.

King. Gloucester, 'tis true that we are in great
    danger;
The greater therefore should our courage be.
Good morrow, brother Bedford. God Almighty!
There is some soul of goodness in things evil,
Would men observingly distill it out.   5
For our bad neighbor makes us early stirrers,
Which is both healthful and good husbandry.
Besides, they are our outward consciences
And preachers to us all, admonishing
That we should dress us fairly for our end.   10
Thus may we gather honey from the weed
And make a moral of the divel himself.

Enter Erpingham.

Good morrow, old Sir Thomas Erpingham.
A good soft pillow for that good white head

50–2 With . . . Agincourt N. 50 foils rapiers. 51 dispos'd set
forth. 53 Minding imagining. 3 Good F *God* N. 7 husbandry
economy, management. 8 they *things evil* (l. 4) or the French.
10 dress us fairly prepare ourselves properly. 12 make . . . of
find a moral lesson in. SD Erpingham N.

Were better than a churlish turf of France.   15
  Erpingham. Not so, my liege. This lodging likes me
    better,
Since I may say 'Now lie I like a king.'
  King. 'Tis good for men to love their present pains
Upon example; so the spirit is eas'd.
And when the mind is quick'ned, out of doubt   20
The organs, though defunct and dead before,
Break up their drowsy grave and newly move
With casted slough and fresh legerity.
Lend me thy cloak, Sir Thomas. Brothers both,
Commend me to the princes in our camp.   25
Do my good morrow to them, and anon
Desire them all to my pavilion.
  Gloucester. We shall, my liege.
  Erpingham. Shall I attend your grace?
  King.   No, my good knight.
Go with my brothers to my lords of England.   30
I and my bosom must debate awhile,
And then I would no other company.
  Erpingham. The Lord in heaven bless thee, noble
    Harry!   *Exeunt [all but the King]*.
  King. God-a-mercy, old heart! Thou speak'st cheer-
    fully.

Enter Pistol.

  Pistol. Qui va là?   35
  King. A friend.
  Pistol. Discuss unto me, art thou officer,

15 **churlish** niggardly, rough. 16 **likes** pleases. 19 **Upon example**
i.e. knowing others have endured the same troubles. 23 **casted**
slough skin cast off. **legerity** nimbleness. 26 **Do** convey. **anon**
immediately. 27 **pavilion** four syllables. 34 **God-a-mercy** many
thanks. 35 **Qui va là** who goes there? N.

Or art thou base, common, and popular?

King. I am a gentleman of a company.

Pistol. Trail'st thou the puissant pike?   40

King. Even so. What are you?

Pistol. As good a gentleman as the emperor.

King. Then you are a better than the king.

Pistol. The king's a bawcock and a heart of gold,

A lad of life, an imp of fame,   45

Of parents good, of fist most valiant.

I kiss his dirty shoe, and from heartstring

I love the lovely bully. What is thy name?

King. Harry le Roy.

Pistol. Le Roy? A Cornish name. Art thou of Cor-

    nish crew?   50

King. No, I am a Welshman.

Pistol. Know'st thou Fluellen?

King. Yes.

Pistol. Tell him I'll knock his leek about his pate

Upon Saint Davy's day.   55

King. Do not you wear your dagger in your cap

that day, lest he knock that about yours.

Pistol. Art thou his friend?

King. And his kinsman too.

Pistol. The figo for thee then!   60

King. I thank you. God be with you!

Pistol. My name is Pistol call'd.   *Exit. Manet King.*

King. It sorts well with your fierceness.

38 **popular** one of the common people. 39 **gentleman . . . company** a gentleman volunteer, or a soldier on probation for promotion. 40 **Trail'st . . . pike** are you in the infantry? **puissant** powerful. **pike** long, heavy lance. 44 **bawcock** fine fellow. 45 **imp** child, scion. 51 **Welshman** the king was born at Monmouth, on the Welsh border. 54 **leek** vegetable related to the onion; the national emblem of the Welsh. 60 **figo** see III.6.58 N. 63 **sorts** fits.

Enter Fluellen and Gower.

Gower. Captain Fluellen!   64

Fluellen. So! in the name of Jesu Christ, speak fewer! It is the greatest admiration in the universal world, when the true and aunchient prerogatifes and laws of the wars is not kept. If you would take the pains but to examine the wars of Pompey the Great, you shall find, I warrant you, that there is no tiddle-taddle nor pibble-pabble in Pompey's camp. I warrant you, you shall find the ceremonies of the wars, and the cares of it, and the forms of it, and the sobriety of it, and the modesty of it, to be otherwise.

Gower. Why, the enemy is loud. You hear him all night.   76

Fluellen. If the enemy is an ass and a fool and a prating coxcomb, is it meet, think you, that we should also, look you, be an ass and a fool and a prating coxcomb, in your own conscience now?   80

Gower. I will speak lower.

Fluellen. I pray you and beseech you that you will.
Exeunt [*Gower and Fluellen*].

King. Though it appear a little out of fashion,
There is much care and valor in this Welshman.   84

Enter three Soldiers, John Bates, Alexander Court, and Michael Williams.

Court. Brother John Bates, is not that the morning which breaks yonder?

---

66 **fewer** F; many editors give *lower* (Q3); Q *lewer*. 66 **admiration** wonder. 67 **prerogatifes** prerogatives, laws. 71 **Pompey's camp** N. 74 **modesty** moderation. 83 **out of fashion** out of the ordinary, quaint.

Bates. I think it be, but we have no great cause to desire the approach of day.

Williams. We see yonder the beginning of the day, but I think we shall never see the end of it. Who goes there?   91

King. A friend.

Williams. Under what captain serve you?

King. Under Sir Thomas Erpingham.

Williams. A good old commander and a most kind gentleman. I pray you, what thinks he of our estate?

King. Even as men wrack'd upon a sand, that look to be wash'd off the next tide.   98

Bates. He hath not told his thought to the king?

King. No, nor it is not meet he should. For though I speak it to you, I think the king is but a man, as I am. The violet smells to him as it doth to me; the element shows to him as it doth to me; all his senses have but human conditions. His ceremonies laid by, in his nakedness he appears but a man. And though his affections are higher mounted than ours, yet when they stoop, they stoop with the like wing. Therefore, when he sees reason of fears, as we do, his fears, out of doubt, be of the same relish as ours are. Yet in reason no man should possess him with any appearance of fear, lest he, by showing it, should dishearten his army.   112

Bates. He may show what outward courage he will, but I believe, as cold a night as 'tis, he could wish

94 Thomas F *Iohn.* 96 estate condition. 97 wrack'd wrecked. sand sand bar. 100 meet fitting. 103 element shows sky appears. 104 conditions characteristics. ceremonies symbols of state. 106 affections . . . mounted desires soar higher. 107 stoop sweep down (image from falconry). 109 out of doubt without doubt. be . . . relish i.e. taste the same. 110 possess him take possession of him.

himself in Thames up to the neck. And so I would he were, and I by him, at all adventures, so we were quit here.

King. By my troth, I will speak my conscience of the king. I think he would not wish himself anywhere but where he is.   120

Bates. Then I would he were here alone. So should he be sure to be ransomed, and a many poor men's lives saved.

King. I dare say you love him not so ill to wish him here alone, howsoever you speak this to feel other men's minds. Methinks I could not die anywhere so contented as in the king's company, his cause being just and his quarrel honorable.   128

Williams. That's more than we know.

Bates. Ay, or more than we should seek after, for we know enough if we know we are the king's subjects. If his cause be wrong, our obedience to the king wipes the crime of it out of us.   133

Williams. But if the cause be not good, the king himself hath a heavy reckoning to make when all those legs and arms and heads chopp'd off in a battle shall join together at the latter day and cry all 'We died at such a place'—some swearing, some crying for a surgeon, some upon their wives left poor behind them, some upon the debts they owe, some upon their children rawly left. I am afeard there are few die well that die in a battle, for how can they charitably dispose of anything when blood is their

116 **at all adventures** at all hazards. 117 **quit** finished with this job. 118 **conscience** inner thoughts. 125 **feel** test. 137 **latter day** judgment day. 139 **some upon** i.e. crying out the names of. 141 **rawly left** poorly provided for. 142 **die well** i.e. who die a Christian death. 143 **charitably . . . anything** settle anything in a spirit of charity.

argument? Now if these men do not die well, it will
be a black matter for the king that led them to it,
who to disobey were against all proportion of subjection.   147

King. So, if a son that is by his father sent about
merchandise do sinfully miscarry upon the sea, the
imputation of his wickedness, by your rule, should
be imposed upon his father that sent him. Or if a
servant under his master's command transporting a
sum of money be assailed by robbers and die in many
irreconcil'd iniquities, you may call the business of
the master the author of the servant's damnation.
But this is not so. The king is not bound to answer
the particular endings of his soldiers, the father of
his son, nor the master of his servant. For they purpose not their death when they purpose their services. Besides, there is no king, be his cause never so
spotless, if it come to the arbitrement of swords, can
try it out with all unspotted soldiers. Some peradventure have on them the guilt of premeditated and contrived murther; some, of beguiling virgins with the
broken seals of perjury; some, making the wars their
bulwark, that have before gored the gentle bosom of
peace with pillage and robbery. Now if these men
have defeated the law and outrun native punishment,
though they can outstrip men, they have no wings

146–7 **proportion of subjection** proper behavior for subjects.
148–9 **about merchandise** on a trading voyage. 149 **sinfully
miscarry** die in his sins. 154 **irreconcil'd iniquities** sins not con-
fessed and atoned for. 156 **answer** answer for. 161 **arbitrement**
decision. 162 **unspotted** sinless. 163–4 **contrived** deliberately
planned. 166 **bulwark** defense; excuse for plundering. 168 **outrun
. . . punishment** escaped punishment in their own country.

to fly from God. War is his beadle, war is his vengeance, so that here men are punish'd for beforebreach of the king's laws in now the king's quarrel. Where they feared the death, they have borne life away, and where they would be safe, they perish. Then if they die unprovided, no more is the king guilty of their damnation than he was before guilty of those impieties for the which they are now visited. Every subject's duty is the king's, but every subject's soul is his own. Therefore should every soldier in the wars do as every sick man in his bed—wash every mote out of his conscience. And dying so, death is to him advantage, or not dying, the time was blessedly lost wherein such preparation was gained. And in him that escapes, it were not sin to think that, making God so free an offer, he let him outlive that day to see his greatness and to teach others how they should prepare. 187

Williams. 'Tis certain every man that dies ill, the ill upon his own head—the king is not to answer it.

Bates. I do not desire he should answer for me, and yet I determine to fight lustily for him. 191

King. I myself heard the king say he would not be ransom'd.

Williams. Ay, he said so to make us fight cheerfully. But when our throats are cut, he may be ransom'd and we ne'er the wiser. 196

King. If I live to see it, I will never trust his word after.

170 **beadle** parish officer who arrested and administered punishment. 171–2 **before-** . . . **now** previous . . . what is now. 173–4 **Where** . . . **perish** see Matthew 16:25. 175 **unprovided** unprepared for death. 177 **visited** i.e. with punishment from God. 181 **mote** tiniest spot; F *Moth.* 185 **offer** i.e. of his soul. 191 **lustily** vigorously.

Williams. You pay him then! That's a perilous shot out of an elder-gun, that a poor and a private displeasure can do against a monarch! You may as well go about to turn the sun to ice with fanning in his face with a peacock's feather. You'll never trust his word after! Come, 'tis a foolish saying.   204

King. Your reproof is something too round. I should be angry with you if the time were convenient.

Williams. Let it be a quarrel between us if you live.

King. I embrace it.

Williams. How shall I know thee again?   210

King. Give me any gage of thine, and I will wear it in my bonnet. Then if ever thou dar'st acknowledge it, I will make it my quarrel.

Williams. Here's my glove. Give me another of thine.   215

King. There.

Williams. This will I also wear in my cap. If ever thou come to me and say, after tomorrow, 'This is my glove,' by this hand, I will take thee a box on the ear.   220

King. If ever I live to see it, I will challenge it.

Williams. Thou dar'st as well be hang'd.

King. Well, I will do it, though I take thee in the king's company.

Williams. Keep thy word. Fare thee well.   225

Bates. Be friends, you English fools, be friends. We have French quarrels enow, if you could tell how to reckon.

---

199 **pay him** give him what he deserves. 200 **elder-gun** popgun. 205 **round** outspoken. 211 **gage** pledge. 219 **take** give. 227 **enow** enough.

King. Indeed, the French may lay twenty French
crowns to one they will beat us, for they bear them
on their shoulders. But it is no English treason to
cut French crowns, and tomorrow the king himself
will be a clipper.   *Exeunt Soldiers.*
Upon the king! Let us our lives, our souls,
Our debts, our careful wives,   235
Our children, and our sins lay on the king!
We must bear all. O, hard condition,
Twin-born with greatness, subject to the breath
Of every fool, whose sense no more can feel
But his own wringing! What infinite heartsease   240
Must kings neglect that private men enjoy!
And what have kings that privates have not too,
Save ceremony, save general ceremony?
And what art thou, thou idol Ceremony?
What kind of god art thou, that suffer'st more   245
Of mortal griefs than do thy worshipers?
What are thy rents? What are thy comings-in?
O Ceremony, show me but thy worth!
What is thy soul of adoration?
Art thou ought else but place, degree, and form,
Creating awe and fear in other men?   251
Wherein thou art less happy being fear'd
Than they in fearing.
What drink'st thou oft instead of homage sweet
But poison'd flattery? O, be sick, great greatness,
And bid thy ceremony give thee cure!   256
Think'st thou the fiery fever will go out

229–33 Indeed . . . clipper N. 233 Exeunt Soldiers F puts after
l. 228. 235 careful full of care. 237–41 We must . . . enjoy N.
239 sense sensibility. 240 wringing suffering. 241 neglect forego.
243 ceremony accessory or symbol of state. 247 comings-in
income. 249 soul of adoration that central virtue which makes
people adore thee N. 250 form formality.

With titles blown from adulation?
Will it give place to flexure and low bending?
Canst thou, when thou command'st the beggar's
  knee,   260
Command the health of it? No, thou proud dream,
That play'st so subtly with a king's repose.
I am a king that find thee, and I know
'Tis not the balm, the scepter, and the ball,
The sword, the mace, the crown imperial,   265
The intertissu'd robe of gold and pearl,
The farced title running 'fore the king,
The throne he sits on, nor the tide of pomp
That beats upon the high shore of this world—
No, not all these, thrice-gorgeous Ceremony,   270
Not all these, laid in bed majestical,
Can sleep so soundly as the wretched slave
Who, with a body fill'd and vacant mind,
Gets him to rest cramm'd with distressful bread,
Never sees horrid night, the child of hell,   275
But like a lackey, from the rise to set,
Sweats in the eye of Phoebus, and all night
Sleeps in Elysium. Next day after dawn,
Doth rise and help Hyperion to his horse
And follows so the ever-running year   280
With profitable labor to his grave.
And, but for ceremony, such a wretch,

257–8 **Think'st . . . adulation** Can the empty titles of flattery
blow out the fire of a fever? 259 **give place to** retire before.
flexure bending the knee. 263 **find thee** find thee out. 264 **balm**
holy oil with which kings are anointed. **scepter** golden rod held
by a king. **ball** the globe carried as a sign of sovereignty. 265
mace symbolizes the power to strike down offenders. 266 **intertissu'd** interwoven. 267 **farced** stuffed (with pompous phrases).
274 **distressful** hard-earned. 277 **Phoebus** the sun. 278 **Elysium**
Paradise. 279 **Hyperion** the sun.

Winding up days with toil and nights with sleep,
Had the forehand and vantage of a king.
The slave, a member of the country's peace,   285
Enjoys it, but in gross brain little wots
What watch the king keeps to maintain the peace,
Whose hours the peasant best advantages.

Enter Erpingham.

Erpingham. My lord, your nobles, jealous of your
          absence,   289
Seek through your camp to find you.
King.   Good old knight,
Collect them all together at my tent.
I'll be before thee.
Erpingham.   I shall do't, my lord.   *Exit.*
King. O God of battles, steel my soldiers' hearts,
Possess them not with fear! Take from them now
The sense of reck'ning, if th' opposed numbers   295
Pluck their hearts from them. Not today, O Lord,
O, not today, think not upon the fault
My father made in compassing the crown!
I Richard's body have interred new
And on it have bestow'd more contrite tears   300
Than from it issu'd forced drops of blood.
Five hundred poor I have in yearly pay,
Who twice a day their wither'd hands hold up
Toward heaven, to pardon blood. And I have built

283 **Winding up** occupying and crowning. 284 **forehand** upper
hand. 285 **member** sharer. 286 **gross** dull. **wots** knows. 288 **best
advantages** turns to the greatest profit. 289 **jealous of** apprehen-
sive about. 295 **sense of** faculty for. **reck'ning, if** N. 296–309
Not today . . . pardon N. 298 **compassing** getting possession of.

Two chantries where the sad and solemn priests   305
Sing still for Richard's soul. More will I do,
Though all that I can do is nothing worth,
Since that my penitence comes after all,
Imploring pardon.

Enter Gloucester.

Gloucester. My liege!   310
  King. My brother Gloucester's voice? Ay.
I know thy errand, I will go with thee.
The day, my friends, and all things stay for me.
                                                Exeunt.

SCENE 2

*Enter the Dolphin, Orleans, Rambures, and
Beaumont.*

Orleans. The sun doth gild our armor. Up, my
  lords!
Dolphin. Montez à cheval! My horse! Varlet! La-
  quais! Ha!
Orleans. O brave spirit!
Dolphin. Via! les eaux et la terre.
Orleans. Rien puis? L'air et le feu.   5

305 **chantries** chapels where priests sing masses for the dead. **sad**
grave. 306 **still** continuously. 313 **friends** F *friend*. SD **Beaumont**
does not speak, and appears here only. 1 **armor. Up** F *Armour vp.*
2 **Montez à cheval** To horse! **Varlet** valet; F *Verlot.* **Laquais**
lackey, servant. 4-6 **Via . . . Ciel** Away, water and earth./
Nothing more? Air and fire./Heavens!

Dolphin. Ciel! Cousin Orleans.

Enter Constable.

Now, my Lord Constable?

   Constable. Hark how our steeds for present service neigh!

   Dolphin. Mount them and make incision in their hides,

That their hot blood may spin in English eyes   10
And dout them with superfluous courage, ha!

   Rambures. What, will you have them weep our horses' blood?

How shall we then behold their natural tears?

Enter Messenger.

   Messenger. The English are embattl'd, you French peers.

   Constable. To horse, you gallant princes, straight to horse!   15

Do but behold yon poor and starved band,
And your fair show shall suck away their souls,
Leaving them but the shales and husks of men.
There is not work enough for all our hands,
Scarce blood enough in all their sickly veins   20
To give each naked curtal ax a stain,
That our French gallants shall today draw out
And sheathe for lack of sport. Let us but blow on them,
The vapor of our valor will o'erturn them.

8 present immediate. 9 make incision i.e. with spurs. 10 spin in
gush forth into. 11 dout put out; F *doubt.* courage thought to
reside in the blood. 14 embattl'd drawn up in battle formation.
17 fair show splendid appearance. 18 shales shells. 21 curtal ax
cutlass, short curved sword used by horsemen when the lance is
broken.

'Tis positive 'gainst all exceptions, lords,   25
That our superfluous lackeys and our peasants,
Who in unnecessary action swarm
About our squares of battle, were enow
To purge this field of such a hilding foe,
Though we upon this mountain's basis by   30
Took stand for idle speculation.
But that our honors must not. What's to say?
A very little little let us do,
And all is done. Then let the trumpets sound
The tucket sonance and the note to mount,   35
For our approach shall so much dare the field
That England shall couch down in fear and yield.

Enter Grandpré.

Grandpré. Why do you stay so long, my lords of
      France?
Yon island carrions, desperate of their bones,
Ill-favoredly become the morning field.   40
Their ragged curtains poorly are let loose,
And our air shakes them passing scornfully.
Big Mars seems bankrout in their beggar'd host
And faintly through a rusty beaver peeps.
The horsemen sit like fixed candlesticks   45
With torch staves in their hand, and their poor jades
Lob down their heads, dropping the hides and hips,

25 **positive** . . . **exceptions** certain against all objections. **'gainst**
F *against.* 28 **enow** enough. 29 **hilding** worthless. 31 **for** . . .
speculation as idle onlookers. 35 **tucket sonance** trumpet call.
36 **dare** dazzle, frighten. 37 **couch** crouch. 39 **carrions** carcasses.
desperate of without hope of saving. 40 **Ill-favoredly become** are
ugly or incongruous upon. 41 **curtains** banners. 42 **passing** very.
43 **bankrout** bankrupt. 44 **beaver** the movable part of the helmet.
45 **candlesticks** figures of men on ornamental candlesticks. 47
Lob hang.

The gum down-roping from their pale-dead eyes,
And in their pale dull mouths the gimmal'd bit
Lies foul with chaw'd grass, still and motionless. 50
And their executors, the knavish crows,
Fly o'er them all, impatient for their hour.
Description cannot suit itself in words
To demonstrate the life of such a battle
In life so liveless as it shows itself. 55
   Constable. They have said their prayers, and they
     stay for death.
   Dolphin. Shall we go send them dinners and fresh
     suits
And give their fasting horses provender,
And after fight with them? 59
   Constable. I stay but for my guidon. To the field!
I will the banner from a trumpet take
And use it for my haste. Come, come away!
The sun is high, and we outwear the day.   *Exeunt.*

SCENE 3

*Enter Gloucester, Bedford, Exeter, Erpingham with
   all his host, Salisbury, and Westmoreland.*

   Gloucester. Where is the king?

48 **down-roping** dangling down like rope. 49 **gimmal'd** jointed;
often read *gimmal;* F *Iymold.* 51 **executors** i.e. those who will
have the disposal of what is left of their bodies. 52 **them all,
impatient** F; many editors read *them, all impatient.* 53 **suit . . .
words** clothe itself in adequate language. 54 **demonstrate . . .
battle** depict such an army to the life. 55 **liveless** lifeless; see
III.6.8–9 N. 60 **guidon** standard; F *Guard:on.* 61 **banner** streamer
fastened to a trumpet. 63 **outwear** wear out.

Bedford. The king himself is rode to view their
    battle.
Westmoreland. Of fighting men they have full three-
    score thousand.
Exeter. There's five to one; besides, they all are
    fresh.
Salisbury. God's arm strike with us! 'Tis a fearful
    odds.   5
God bye you, princes all. I'll to my charge.
If we no more meet till we meet in heaven,
Then joyfully, my noble Lord of Bedford,
My dear Lord Gloucester, and my good Lord Exeter,
And my kind kinsman, warriors all, adieu!   10
   Bedford. Farwell, good Salisbury, and good luck
    go with thee!
   Exeter. Farwell, kind lord. Fight valiantly today.
And yet I do thee wrong to mind thee of it,
For thou art fram'd of the firm truth of valor.
                              [Exit Salisbury.]
   Bedford. He is as full of valor as of kindness,   15
Princely in both.

Enter the King.

   Westmoreland. O, that we now had here
But one ten thousand of those men in England
That do no work today!
   King.   What's he that wishes so?
My cousin Westmoreland? No, my fair cousin.
If we are mark'd to die, we are enow   20
To do our country loss, and if to live,

2 **battle** army lines. 3–4 **threescore . . . to one** from Holinshed,
who says 'six times as manie.' 6 **God . . . you** most editors read
God be wi' you; F *God buy' you.* **charge** command. 11–14 **Farwell
. . . valor** farewell, etc. N. 13 **mind** remind. 14 **fram'd** made.
16–18 **O . . . today** N.

The fewer men, the greater share of honor.
God's will! I pray thee wish not one man more.
By Jove, I am not covetous for gold,
Nor care I who doth feed upon my cost.   25
It yearns me not if men my garments wear;
Such outward things dwell not in my desires.
But if it be a sin to covet honor,
I am the most offending soul alive.   29
No, faith, my coz, wish not a man from England.
God's peace! I would not lose so great an honor
As one man more, methinks, would share from me
For the best hope I have. O, do not wish one more!
Rather proclaim it, Westmoreland, through my host
That he which hath no stomach to this fight,   35
Let him depart. His passport shall be made
And crowns for convoy put into his purse.
We would not die in that man's company
That fears his fellowship to die with us.
This day is call'd the feast of Crispian.   40
He that outlives this day and comes safe home
Will stand a-tiptoe when this day is nam'd
And rouse him at the name of Crispian.
He that shall see this day and live old age
Will yearly on the vigil feast his neighbors   45
And say 'Tomorrow is Saint Crispian.'
Then will he strip his sleeve and show his scars,
[And say 'These wounds I had on Crispin's day.']
Old men forget; yet all shall be forgot,
But he'll remember with advantages   50

25 upon at. 26 yearns grieves. 28–9 But if . . . alive N. 37
convoy traveling expenses. 39 fears . . . us fears to share death
with us. 40 Crispian N. 44 live F; live to N. 45 vigil eve of a Christian festival. 48 And say . . . day Q; not in F. 50 advantages
exaggerations.

What feats he did that day. Then shall our names,
Familiar in his mouth as household words—
Harry the King, Bedford and Exeter,
Warwick and Talbot, Salisbury and Gloucester—
Be in their flowing cups freshly rememb'red.   55
This story shall the good man teach his son.
And Crispin Crispian shall ne'er go by
From this day to the ending of the world,
But we in it shall be remembered—
We few, we happy few, we band of brothers.   60
For he today that sheds his blood with me
Shall be my brother. Be he ne'er so vile,
This day shall gentle his condition.
And gentlemen in England now abed   64
Shall think themselves accurs'd they were not here,
And hold their manhoods cheap whiles any speaks
That fought with us upon Saint Crispin's day.

Enter Salisbury.

Salisbury. My sovereign lord, bestow yourself with
    speed.
The French are bravely in their battles set
And will with all expedience charge on us.   70
    King. All things are ready if our minds be so.
    Westmoreland. Perish the man whose mind is back-
        ward now!
    King. Thou dost not wish more help from England,
        coz?
    Westmoreland. God's will, my liege! Would you and
        I alone,

62 vile of low birth. 63 **gentle . . . condition** give him the rank
of a gentleman. 68 **bestow yourself** take up your position. 69
bravely in splendid array. **battles** lines of battle. 70 **expedience**
haste.

Without more help, could fight this royal battle! 75
  King. Why, now thou hast unwish'd five thousand
    men,
Which likes me better than to wish us one.
You know your places. God be with you all!

Tucket. Enter Montjoy.

  Montjoy. Once more I come to know of thee, King
    Harry,
If for thy ransom thou wilt now compound 80
Before thy most assured overthrow.
For certainly thou art so near the gulf
Thou needs must be englutted. Besides, in mercy,
The Constable desires thee thou wilt mind
Thy followers of repentance, that their souls 85
May make a peaceful and a sweet retire
From off these fields, where, wretches, their poor
    bodies
Must lie and fester.
  King.   Who hath sent thee now?
  Montjoy. The Constable of France.
  King. I pray thee bear my former answer back. 90
Bid them achieve me and then sell my bones.
Good God! Why should they mock poor fellows thus?
The man that once did sell the lion's skin
While the beast liv'd was kill'd with hunting him.
A many of our bodies shall no doubt 95
Find native graves, upon the which, I trust,
Shall witness live in brass of this day's work.
And those that leave their valiant bones in France,

77 **likes** pleases. 80 **compound** make terms. 82 **gulf** whirlpool.
83 **englutted** swallowed up. 84 **mind** remind. 91 **achieve** capture,
kill. 96 **native** i.e. in England. 97 **in brass** i.e. a memorial tablet
in a church.

Dying like men, though buried in your dunghills,
They shall be fam'd. For there the sun shall greet
    them   100
And draw their honors reeking up to heaven,
Leaving their earthly parts to choke your clime,
The smell whereof shall breed a plague in France.
Mark then abounding valor in our English,
That being dead, like to the bullet's crasing,   105
Break out into a second course of mischief,
Killing in relapse of mortality.
Let me speak proudly. Tell the Constable
We are but warriors for the working day.
Our gayness and our gilt are all besmirch'd   110
With rainy marching in the painful field.
There's not a piece of feather in our host—
Good argument, I hope, we will not fly—
And time hath worn us into slovenry.
But, by the mass, our hearts are in the trim,   115
And my poor soldiers tell me, yet ere night
They'll be in fresher robes, or they will pluck
The gay new coats o'er the French soldiers' heads
And turn them out of service. If they do this—
As, if God please, they shall—my ransom then   120
Will soon be levied. Herald, save thou thy labor.
Come thou no more for ransom, gentle herald.
They shall have none, I swear, but these my joints,
Which if they have as I will leave 'em them,
Shall yield them little, tell the Constable.   125

105 **crasing** variant form of 'grazing,' rebounding. 107 **relapse of**
mortality renewed power to kill; decomposition. 109 **working day**
i.e. strictly for business. 112 **feather** i.e. in plumes on the helmets.
113 argument proof. 119 **turn . . . service** deprive them of their
coats as if they were servants wearing their master's livery.
124 'em F *vm.*

Montjoy. I shall, King Harry. And so fare thee well.

Thou never shalt hear herald any more.   *Exit.*

King. I fear thou wilt once more come again for a ransom.

Enter York.

York. My lord, most humbly on my knee I beg

The leading of the vaward.   130

King. Take it, brave York. Now, soldiers, march away,

And how thou pleasest, God, dispose the day!

Exeunt.

SCENE 4

Alarum. Excursions. Enter Pistol, French Soldier, Boy.

Pistol. Yield, cur!

French. Je pense que vous êtes le gentilhomme de bonne qualité.

Pistol. Qualtitie calmie custure me! Art thou a gentleman? What is thy name? Discuss.   5

French. O Seigneur Dieu!

Pistol. O Signieur Dew should be a gentleman.

Perpend my words, O Signieur Dew, and mark.

O Signieur Dew, thou diest on point of fox,

128 **thou wilt** read 'thou'lt.' 130 **vaward** vanguard. SD **Alarum** trumpet call to arms. **Excursions** sallies across the stage as if in battle N. 2–3 **Je . . . qualité** I think that you are a gentleman of high rank. 4 **Qualtitie . . . me** N. 7–11 **O . . . ransom** N. 8 **Perpend** ponder. 9 **fox** sword.

Except, O Signieur, thou do give to me   10
Egregious ransom.

French. O, prenez miséricorde! Ayez pitié de moi!

Pistol. Moy shall not serve, I will have forty moys,
Or I will fetch thy rim out at thy throat
In drops of crimson blood.   15

French. Est-il impossible d'échapper la force de ton
bras?

Pistol. Brass, cur?
Thou damned and luxurious mountain goat,
Offer'st me brass?   20

French. O, pardonnez-moi!

Pistol. Say'st thou me so? Is that a ton of moys?
Come hither, boy. Ask me this slave in French
What is his name.

Boy. Écoutez. Comment êtes-vous appelé?   25

French. Monsieur le Fer.

Boy. He says his name is Master Fer.

Pistol. Master Fer! I'll fer him, and firk him, and
ferret him! Discuss the same in French unto him.

Boy. I do not know the French for fer, and ferret,
and firk.   31

Pistol. Bid him prepare, for I will cut his throat.

11 **Egregious** enormous. 12 **O . . . moi** O, have mercy! Have
pity on me! (*moi* was pronounced 'moy'). 13 **Moy** Pistol perhaps
thinks that the Frenchman speaks of a coin, or unit of measure.
14 **Or F** *for.* **rim** diaphragm. 16–17 **Est-il . . . bras** Is it impossible to escape the strength of your arm? 18 **Brass** the *s* in *bras*
was sounded in French of this period. 19 **luxurious** lascivious.
21–2 **pardonnez . . . a ton of** most of Pistol's echoes are of this
sort. 25 **Écoutez . . . appelé** Listen. What is your name? 28 **firk**
beat. 29 **ferret** worry.

French. Que dit-il, monsieur?

Boy. Il me commande à vous dire que vous faites
vous prêt, car ce soldat ici est disposé tout à cette
heure de couper votre gorge.

Pistol. Owy, cuppele gorge, permafoy,   37
Peasant, unless thou give me crowns, brave crowns,
Or mangled shalt thou be by this my sword.

French. O, je vous supplie, pour l'amour de Dieu,
me pardonner! Je suis le gentilhomme de bonne mai-
son. Gardez ma vie, et je vous donnerai deux cents
écus.   43

Pistol. What are his words?

Boy. He prays you to save his life. He is a gentleman of a good house, and for his ransom he will give
you two hundred crowns.

Pistol. Tell him my fury shall abate, and I
The crowns will take.

French. Petit monsieur, que dit-il?   50

Boy. Encore qu'il est contre son jurement de pardonner aucun prisonnier; néanmoins, pour les écus

33–6 **Que . . . gorge** What does he say, sir? *Boy.* He bids me
tell you that you prepare yourself, because this soldier is inclined
to cut your throat at once. 35–6 **à cette heure** N. 37 **Owy . . .
permafoy** Yes, cut your throat, in faith N. 38 **brave** fine. 40–3
O . . . écus O, I beseech you, for the love of God, to pardon me!
I am a gentleman of a good house. Save my life, and I shall give
you two hundred crowns. 50–8 **Petit . . . d'Angleterre** Little sir,
what does he say? *Boy.* [I say] again that it is against his oath
to pardon any prisoner; nevertheless, for the crowns which you
have promised, he is willing to give you your liberty, your freedom. *Frenchman.* On my knees I give you a thousand thanks,
and I consider myself happy that I have fallen into the hands of
a knight, I think, the bravest, the most valiant and distinguished
nobleman in England.

100

que vous l'avez promis, il est content de vous donner
la liberté, le franchisement.   54

French. Sur mes genoux je vous donne mille remer-
cîments, et je m'estime heureux que je suis tombé
entre les mains d'un chevalier, je pense, le plus brave,
vaillant, et très distingué seigneur d'Angleterre.

Pistol. Expound unto me, boy.   59

Boy. He gives you upon his knees a thousand
thanks, and he esteems himself happy that he hath
fall'n into the hands of one (as he thinks) the most
brave, valorous, and thrice-worthy signieur of England.

Pistol. As I suck blood, I will some mercy show!
Follow me.   66

Boy. Suivez-vous le grand capitaine.

      [Exeunt Pistol and French Soldier.]
I did never know so full a voice issue from so empty
a heart. But the saying is true: 'The empty vessel
makes the greatest sound.' Bardolph and Nym had
ten times more valor than this roaring divel i' th'
old play, that everyone may pare his nails with a
wooden dagger, and they are both hang'd. And so
would this be, if he durst steal anything adventur-
ously. I must stay with the lackeys, with the luggage
of our camp. The French might have a good prey
of us, if he knew of it, for there is none to guard it
but boys.   *Exit.*

67 Suivez-vous . . . capitaine Follow the great captain. 69 heart
the seat of courage. 71–3 roaring . . . dagger N. 72 that . . .
his whose.

SCENE 5

Enter Constable, Orleans, Bourbon, Dolphin, and Rambures.

Constable. O diable!

Orleans. O Seigneur! le jour est perdu, tout est perdu!

Dolphin. Mort Dieu! ma vie! all is confounded, all!
Reproach and everlasting shame
Sits mocking in our plumes.   *A short alarum.*
O méchante fortune! Do not run away.   6

Constable. Why, all our ranks are broke.

Dolphin. O, perdurable shame! Let's stab ourselves.
Be these the wretches that we play'd at dice for?

Orleans. Is this the king we sent to for his ransom?

Bourbon. Shame, and eternal shame, nothing but
shame!   11
Let us die in honor. Once more back again!
And he that will not follow Bourbon now,
Let him go hence, and with his cap in hand,
Like a base pander hold the chamber door   15
Whilst by a slave no gentler than my dog
His fairest daughter is contaminated.

Constable. Disorder that hath spoil'd us, friend us
now!
Let us on heaps go offer up our lives.

Orleans. We are enow yet living in the field   20

2 O . . . perdu O Lord! the day is lost, all is lost! 3 Mort . . . vie
F *Mor Dieu ma vie;* see III.5.11. confounded ruined. 6 méchante
wicked, spiteful. 8 perdurable everlasting. 9 Be are. 12 die in
honor. Once N. 16 by a slave Q; F *a base slaue.* 18 spoil'd ruined.
friend befriend. 19 on heaps in crowds.

To smother up the English in our throngs,
If any order might be thought upon.
  Bourbon. The divel take order now! I'll to the
    throng.
Let life be short, else shame will be too long. *Exeunt.*

SCENE 6

*Alarum. Enter the King and his train, [Exeter, and
others,] with Prisoners.*

  King. Well have we done, thrice valiant country-
    men!
But all's not done; yet keep the French the field.
  Exeter. The Duke of York commends him to your
    majesty.
  King. Lives he, good uncle? Thrice within this hour
I saw him down, thrice up again and fighting.   5
From helmet to the spur all blood he was.
  Exeter. In which array, brave soldier, doth he lie,
Larding the plain, and by his bloody side,
Yoke-fellow to his honor-owing wounds,
The noble Earl of Suffolk also lies.   10
Suffolk first died, and York, all haggled over,
Comes to him where in gore he lay insteep'd,
And takes him by the beard, kisses the gashes
That bloodily did yawn upon his face,
And cries aloud 'Tarry, my cousin Suffolk!   15
My soul shall thine keep company to heaven.

3 **commends him** sends his respects. 8 **Larding** enriching. 9 **honor-owing** possessing honor, honorable. 11 **haggled** hacked. 12 **insteep'd** stained. 14–15 **face, And** Q; F *face. He.*

Tarry, sweet soul, for mine, then fly abreast,
As in this glorious and well-foughten field
We kept together in our chivalry.'
Upon these words I came and cheer'd him up.   20
He smil'd me in the face, raught me his hand,
And with a feeble gripe says 'Dear my lord,
Commend my service to my sovereign.'
So did he turn, and over Suffolk's neck
He threw his wounded arm and kiss'd his lips,   25
And so espous'd to death, with blood he seal'd
A testament of noble-ending love.
The pretty and sweet manner of it forc'd
Those waters from me which I would have stopp'd.
But I had not so much of man in me,   30
And all my mother came into mine eyes
And gave me up to tears.
   King.   I blame you not,
For, hearing this, I must perforce compound
With mistful eyes, or they will issue too.   *Alarum.*
But hark! What new alarum is this same?   35
The French have reinforc'd their scatter'd men.
Then every soldier kill his prisoners.
Give the word through.   *Exeunt.*

21 **raught** reached. 22 **gripe** grip. 28 **pretty** lovely. 31 **mother** the
more tender part of me. 33 **compound** come to terms. 34 **issue**
flow. **Alarum** trumpet call to arms. 37 **kill his prisoners** i.e. so
that the prisoners could not revolt and kill their captors N.

SCENE 7

Enter Fluellen and Gower.

Fluellen. Kill the poys and the luggage! 'Tis expressly against the law of arms. 'Tis as arrant a piece of knavery, mark you now, as can be offert. In your conscience, now, is it not? 4

Gower. 'Tis certain there's not a boy left alive, and the cowardly rascals that ran from the battle ha' done this slaughter. Besides, they have burned and carried away all that was in the king's tent, wherefore the king most worthily hath caus'd every soldier to cut his prisoner's throat. O, 'tis a gallant king! 11

Fluellen. Ay, he was porn at Monmouth, Captain Gower. What call you the town's name where Alexander the Pig was born?

Gower. Alexander the Great. 15

Fluellen. Why, I pray you, is not 'pig' great? The pig, or the great, or the mighty, or the huge, or the magnanimous are all one reckonings, save the phrase is a little variations.

Gower. I think Alexander the Great was born in Macedon. His father was called Philip of Macedon, as I take it. 22

Fluellen. I think it is Macedon where Alexander is porn. I tell you, captain, if you look in the maps of the 'orld, I warrant you sall find, in the comparisons between Macedon and Monmouth, that the situations, look you, is both alike. There is a river in Macedon,

IV.7 F wrongly heads this *Actus Quartus.* 18 **magnanimous** great souled.

and there is also moreover a river at Monmouth. It
is call'd Wye at Monmouth, but it is out of my
prains what is the name of the other river. But 'tis
all one; 'tis alike as my fingers is to my fingers, and
there is salmons in both. If you mark Alexander's
life well, Harry of Monmouth's life is come after it
indifferent well, for there is figures in all things.
Alexander, God knows, and you know, in his rages,
and his furies, and his wraths, and his cholers, and
his moods, and his displeasures, and his indignations,
and also being a little intoxicates in his prains, did
in his ales and his angers, look you, kill his best
friend, Cleitus.   40

Gower. Our king is not like him in that. He never
kill'd any of his friends.

Fluellen. It is not well done, mark you now, to take
the tales out of my mouth, ere it is made and finished.
I speak but in the figures and comparisons of it. As
Alexander kill'd his friend Cleitus, being in his ales
and his cups, so also Harry Monmouth, being in his
right wits and his good judgments, turn'd away the
fat knight with the great-belly doublet. He was full
of jests, and gipes, and knaveries, and mocks. I
have forgot his name.   51

Gower. Sir John Falstaff.

Fluellen. That is he. I'll tell you, there is good men
porn at Monmouth.

Gower. Here comes his majesty.   55

33–4 is . . . well takes after it fairly well. 34 figures prototypes,
analogies, significance. 40 Cleitus one of the generals of Alexander
the Great. 49 great-belly doublet a long waistcoat. 50 gipes jibes.
52 Falstaff see the famous rejection scene (2 *Henry IV*, V.5).

Alarum. Enter King Harry and Bourbon with Pris-
oners, [Warwick, Gloucester, Exeter, and others].
Flourish.

King. I was not angry since I came to France
Until this instant. Take a trumpet, herald.
Ride thou unto the horsemen on yon hill.
If they will fight with us, bid them come down,
Or void the field. They do offend our sight.   60
If they'll do neither, we will come to them
And make them skirr away as swift as stones
Enforced from the old Assyrian slings.
Besides, we'll cut the throats of those we have,
And not a man of them that we shall take   65
Shall taste our mercy. Go and tell them so.

Enter Montjoy.

Exeter. Here comes the herald of the French, my
          liege.
Gloucester. His eyes are humbler than they us'd
          to be.
King. How now! What means this, herald? Know'st
          thou not   69
That I have fin'd these bones of mine for ransom?
Com'st thou again for ransom?
Montjoy.   No, great king.
I come to thee for charitable license,
That we may wander o'er this bloody field

SD Bourbon N. 56–66 **I was . . . them so** N. 57 **trumpet** trum-
peter. 60 **void** abandon. 62 **skirr** scurry. 63 **Assyrian slings** see
Judith 9:7. 64–6 **we'll cut . . . mercy** Gower said (ll. 9–10) that
the order given at IV.6.37 was already carried out. 67–91 **Here**
comes . . . Agincourt N. 70 **fin'd** reserved as a fine, fixed as the
price to be paid.

To book our dead, and then to bury them,
To sort our nobles from our common men.   75
For many of our princes—woe the while!—
Lie drown'd and soak'd in mercenary blood.
So do our vulgar drench their peasant limbs
In blood of princes, and their wounded steeds
Fret fetlock-deep in gore and with wild rage   80
Yerk out their armed heels at their dead masters,
Killing them twice. O, give us leave, great king,
To view the field in safety and dispose
Of their dead bodies!
King.   I tell thee truly, herald,
I know not if the day be ours or no,   85
For yet a many of your horsemen peer
And gallop o'er the field.
Montjoy.   The day is yours.
King. Prais'd be God and not our strength for it!
What is this castle call'd that stands hard by?
Montjoy. They call it Agincourt.   90
King. Then call we this the field of Agincourt,
Fought on the day of Crispin Crispianus.
Fluellen. Your grandfather of famous memory, an't
please your majesty, and your great-uncle Edward
the Plack Prince of Wales, as I have read in the
chronicles, fought a most prave pattle here in
France.   97
King. They did, Fluellen.
Fluellen. Your majesty says very true. If your
majesties is rememb'red of it, the Welshmen did good

74 book register. 77 **mercenary blood** blood of average soldiers,
who, unlike the nobles, fight for wages. 78 **vulgar** common soldiers. 79 **and their** F *and with.* 80 **Fret** chafe. 81 **Yerk** kick.
armed spiked. 86 **peer** appear. 93 **grandfather** great-grandfather
(if Edward III is meant). 96 **pattle** the Battle of Crécy. 100–02
Welshmen . . . caps N

service in a garden where leeks did grow, wearing
leeks in their Monmouth caps, which your majesty
know to this hour is an honorable badge of the service. And I do believe your majesty takes no scorn to
wear the leek upon Saint Tavy's Day.   105

King. I wear it for a memorable honor,
For I am Welsh, you know, good countryman.

Fluellen. All the water in Wye cannot wash your
majesty's Welsh plood out of your pody, I can tell
you that. God pless it, and preserve it, as long as it
pleases his grace, and his majesty too!   111

King. Thanks, good my countryman.

Fluellen. By Jeshu, I am your majesty's countryman, I care not who know it! I will confess it to all
the 'orld. I need not to be ashamed of your majesty,
praised be God, so long as your majesty is an honest
man.   117

King. God keep me so!

Enter Williams.

                    Our heralds go with him.
Bring me just notice of the numbers dead
On both our parts. [*Exeunt Heralds with Montjoy.*]
                    Call yonder fellow hither.   120

Exeter. Soldier, you must come to the king.

King. Soldier, why wear'st thou that glove in thy
cap?

Williams. An't please your majesty, 'tis the gage
of one that I should fight withal, if he be alive.

King. An Englishman?   126

Williams. An't please your majesty, a rascal that

---

106 memorable honor honorable memorial. 109 Welsh plood N.
118 God F *Good.* 119-20 Bring . . . parts N. 119 just exact.

swagger'd with me last night, who, if alive and ever dare to challenge this glove, I have sworn to take him a box o' th' ear. Or if I can see my glove in his cap—which he swore as he was a soldier he would wear, if alive—I will strike it out soundly.   132

King. What think you, Captain Fluellen? Is it fit this soldier keep his oath?

Fluellen. He is a craven and a villain else, an't please your majesty, in my conscience.

King. It may be his enemy is a gentleman of great sort, quite from the answer of his degree.   138

Fluellen. Though he be as good a gentleman as the divel is, as Lucifer and Belzebub himself, it is necessary, look your grace, that he keep his vow and his oath. If he be perjur'd, see you now, his reputation is as arrant a villain and a Jacksauce as ever his black shoe trod upon God's ground, and his earth, in my conscience, la!   145

King. Then keep thy vow, sirrah, when thou meet'st the fellow.

Williams. So I will, my liege, as I live.

King. Who serv'st thou under?

Williams. Under Captain Gower, my liege.   150

Fluellen. Gower is a good captain, and is good knowledge and literatured in the wars.

King. Call him hither to me, soldier.

Williams. I will, my liege.   *Exit.*

King. Here, Fluellen, wear thou this favor for me and stick it in thy cap. When Alençon and myself were down together, I pluck'd this glove from his

128 alive F; many editors read *a' live.* 129 take give. 138 quite . . . degree too far above Williams' rank to accept any challenge from him. 143 Jacksauce saucy knave. 143–4 his . . . shoe anyone whose dirty foot.

helm. If any man challenge this, he is a friend to
Alençon and an enemy to our person. If thou encounter any such, apprehend him, an thou dost me
love.   161

Fluellen. Your grace doo's me as great honors as
can be desir'd in the hearts of his subjects. I would
fain see the man, that has but two legs, that shall
find himself aggrief'd at this glove, that is all. But I
would fain see it once, an please God of his grace
that I might see.   167

King. Know'st thou Gower?

Fluellen. He is my dear friend, an please you.

King. Pray thee, go seek him and bring him to my
tent.   171

Fluellen. I will fetch him.   *Exit.*

King. My Lord of Warwick, and my brother Glou-
            cester,
Follow Fluellen closely at the heels.
The glove which I have given him for a favor   175
May haply purchase him a box o' th' ear.
It is the soldier's. I by bargain should
Wear it myself. Follow, good cousin Warwick.
If that the soldier strike him, as I judge
By his blunt bearing he will keep his word,   180
Some sudden mischief may arise of it.
For I do know Fluellen valiant
And, touch'd with choler, hot as gunpowder,
And quickly will return an injury.
Follow, and see there be no harm between them.   185
Go you with me, uncle of Exeter.   *Exeunt.*

160 apprehend arrest. an if. 162 doo's does N. 183 choler anger.
184 injury insult.

SCENE 8

Enter Gower and Williams.

Williams. I warrant it is to knight you, captain.

Enter Fluellen.

Fluellen. God's will and his pleasure, captain, I
beseech you now, come apace to the king. There is
more good toward you peradventure than is in your
knowledge to dream of.   5

Williams. Sir, know you this glove?

Fluellen. Know the glove! I know the glove is a
glove.

Williams. I know this, and thus I challenge it.

Strikes him.

Fluellen. 'Sblood! an arrant traitor as any is in the
universal world, or in France, or in England!   11

Gower. How now, sir! You villain!

Williams. Do you think I'll be forsworn?

Fluellen. Stand away, Captain Gower. I will give
treason his payment into plows, I warrant you.   15

Williams. I am no traitor.

Fluellen. That's a lie in thy throat! I charge you in
his majesty's name, apprehend him. He's a friend of
the Duke Alençon's.   19

Enter Warwick and Gloucester.

Warwick. How now, how now! What's the matter?

Fluellen. My Lord of Warwick, here is—praised be
God for it!—a most contagious treason come to

10 'Sblood by God's blood. **any is** F *anyes.* 13 **be forsworn** break
my oath.

light, look you, as you shall desire in a summer's day.
Here is his majesty.

Enter King and Exeter.

King. How now! What's the matter?   25
Fluellen. My liege, here is a villain and a traitor
that, look your grace, has struck the glove which
your majesty is take out of the helmet of Alençon.
Williams. My liege, this was my glove, here is the
fellow of it. And he that I gave it to in change
promis'd to wear it in his cap. I promis'd to strike
him if he did. I met this man with my glove in his
cap, and I have been as good as my word.   33
Fluellen. Your majesty hear now, saving your majesty's manhood, what an arrant, rascally, beggarly,
lousy knave it is. I hope your majesty is pear me
testimony and witness, and will avouchment, that this
is the glove of Alençon that your majesty is give me,
in your conscience now.   39
King. Give me thy glove, soldier. Look, here is the
    fellow of it.
'Twas I indeed thou promised'st to strike,
And thou hast given me most bitter terms.
Fluellen. An please your majesty, let his neck answer for it, if there is any martial law in the world.
King. How canst thou make me satisfaction?   45
Williams. All offenses, my lord, come from the
heart. Never came any from mine that might offend
your majesty.
King. It was ourself thou didst abuse.   49
Williams. Your majesty came not like yourself. You
appear'd to me but as a common man. Witness the

30 **change** exchange. 37 **avouchment** certify. 42 **terms** words.
43 **An** if it. 44 **martial** F *Marshall.*

night, your garments, your lowliness. And what your
highness suffer'd under that shape, I beseech you
take it for your own fault, and not mine. For had
you been as I took you for, I made no offense. Therefore I beseech your highness pardon me.   56

King. Here, uncle Exeter, fill this glove with crowns
And give it to this fellow. Keep it, fellow,
And wear it for an honor in thy cap
Till I do challenge it. Give him the crowns,   60
And, captain, you must needs be friends with him.

Fluellen. By this day and this light, the fellow has
mettle enough in his belly. Hold, there is twelve pence
for you, and I pray you to serve God, and keep you
out of prawls and prabbles, and quarrels, and dis-
sentions, and I warrant you it is the better for you.

Williams. I will none of your money.   67

Fluellen. It is with a good will. I can tell you it will
serve you to mend your shoes. Come, wherefore
should you be so pashful? Your shoes is not so good.
'Tis a good silling, I warrant you, or I will change it.

Enter [an English] Herald.

King. Now, herald, are the dead numb'red?   72

Herald. Here is the number of the slaught'red
          French.   [*Gives a paper.*]

King. What prisoners of good sort are taken, uncle?

Exeter. Charles Duke of Orleans, nephew to the
          king,
John Duke of Bourbon and Lord Bouciqualt.   76
Of other lords and barons, knights and squires,

65 **prabbles** quarrels. 71 **silling** shilling. 74 **sort** rank. 75–105
Charles . . . twenty both names and phrasing (except l. 100)
are taken from Holinshed. 76 **Bouciqualt** F *Bouchiquald.*

114

Full fifteen hundred, besides common men.

King. This note doth tell me of ten thousand French
That in the field lie slain. Of princes in this number,
And nobles bearing banners, there lie dead   81
One hundred twenty-six. Added to these,
Of knights, esquires, and gallant gentlemen,
Eight thousand and four hundred, of the which
Five hundred were but yesterday dubb'd knights. 85
So that in these ten thousand they have lost
There are but sixteen hundred mercenaries.
The rest are princes, barons, lords, knights, squires,
And gentlemen of blood and quality.
The names of those their nobles that lie dead: 90
Charles Delabreth, High Constable of France,
Jaques of Chatillon, Admiral of France,
The master of the crossbows, Lord Rambures,
Great Master of France, the brave Sir Guichard
        Dolphin,   94
John Duke of Alençon, Anthony Duke of Brabant,
The brother to the Duke of Burgundy,
And Edward Duke of Bar. Of lusty earls,
Grandpré and Roussi, Faulconbridge and Foix,
Beaumont and Marle, Vaudemont and Lestrake.
Here was a royal fellowship of death!   100
Where is the number of our English dead?
                    [*Herald gives another paper.*]
Edward the Duke of York, the Earl of Suffolk,
Sir Richard Kikely, Davy Gam, esquire.
None else of name, and of all other men,

---

79 note list. 81 **bearing banners** i.e. indicating their coats of arms.
87 **mercenaries** common soldiers. 98 **Faulconbridge** F *Faucon-bridge and Foyes;* see III.5.44 N. 99 **Lestrake** Holinshed; F
Lestrale. 103 **Kikely** Holinshed; F *Ketly.* 104 **name** rank.

But five and twenty. O God, thy arm was here! 105
And not to us, but to thy arm alone
Ascribe we all. When, without stratagem,
But in plain shock and even play of battle,
Was ever known so great and little loss
On one part and on th' other? Take it, God, 110
For it is none but thine!

    Exeter.   'Tis wonderful!

    King. Come, go we in procession to the village.
And be it death proclaimed through our host
To boast of this, or take that praise from God
Which is his only. 115

    Fluellen. Is it not lawful, an please your majesty, to
tell how many is kill'd?

    King. Yes, captain, but with this acknowledgment,
That God fought for us. 119

    Fluellen. Yes, my conscience, he did us great good.

    King. Do we all holy rites.
Let there be sung *Non nobis* and *Te Deum*,
The dead with charity enclos'd in clay.
And then to Callice, and to England then, 124
Where ne'er from France arriv'd more happy men.

                         Exeunt.

105 But . . . twenty N. 112 we F *me.* 121 rites F *Rights;* passage is close to Holinshed. 122 **Non . . . Deum** well known psalms. 123 **charity . . . clay** full Christian burial.

116

Act V

Enter Chorus.

Vouchsafe to those that have not read the story
That I may prompt them. And of such as have,
I humbly pray them to admit th' excuse
Of time, of numbers, and due course of things
Which cannot in their huge and proper life   5
Be here presented. Now we bear the king
Toward Callice. Grant him there. There seen,
Heave him away upon your winged thoughts
Athwart the sea. Behold, the English beach
Pales in the flood with men, with wives and boys,   10
Whose shouts and claps outvoice the deep-mouth'd
    sea,
Which like a mighty whiffler 'fore the king
Seems to prepare his way. So let him land
And solemnly see him set on to London.
So swift a pace hath thought that even now   15
You may imagine him upon Blackheath,
Where that his lords desire him to have borne
His bruised helmet and his bended sword
Before him through the city. He forbids it,   19
Being free from vainness and self-glorious pride,

3 excuse omission or scanting of N. 10 Pales in surrounds, bounds.
with wives F2; with not in F. 12 whiffler an officer who goes before
a procession to clear the way. 14 solemnly in state. 16 Blackheath
district south of London. 17 Where that where. 17–22 Where
. . . God N.

117

Giving full trophy, signal, and ostent
Quite from himself to God. But now behold,
In the quick forge and working house of thought,
How London doth pour out her citizens!
The mayor and all his brethren in best sort, 25
Like to the senators of th' antique Rome,
With the plebeians swarming at their heels,
Go forth and fetch their conqu'ring Caesar in;
As, by a lower but loving likelihood,
Were now the general of our gracious empress, 30
As in good time he may, from Ireland coming,
Bringing rebellion broached on his sword,
How many would the peaceful city quit
To welcome him! Much more, and much more cause,
Did they this Harry. Now in London place him—
As yet the lamentation of the French 36
Invites the King of England's stay at home;
The emperor's coming in behalf of France
To order peace between them—and omit
All the occurrences, whatever chanc'd, 40
Till Harry's back return again to France.
There must we bring him, and myself have play'd
The interim, by rememb'ring you 'tis past.
Then brook abridgment, and your eyes advance,
After your thoughts, straight back again to France.
               Exit.

---

21 **trophy** tokens of victory. **signal** sign of victory. **ostent** triumphal show. 25 **in best sort** in finest array. 26 **antique** stressed ´ ̶ . 29 **loving likelihood** affectionate probability; F *by louing*. 30 **general** N. 32 **broached** stuck on a spit, transfixed. 38 **emperor's coming** N. 42–3 **myself . . . interim** i.e. I have told all that has happened between Acts IV (1415) and V (1420). 43 **rememb'ring** reminding. 44 **brook abridgment** put up with our cutting down the story.

118

SCENE 1

Enter Fluellen and Gower.

Gower. Nay, that's right. But why wear you your leek today? Saint Davy's Day is past.

Fluellen. There is occasions and causes why and wherefore in all things. I will tell you asse my friend, Captain Gower. The rascally, scauld, beggarly, lousy, pragging knave Pistol—which you and yourself, and all the world, know to be no petter than a fellow, look you now, of no merits—he is come to me, and prings me pread and salt yesterday, look you, and bid me eat my leek. It was in a place where I could not breed no contention with him. But I will be so bold as to wear it in my cap till I see him once again, and then I will tell him a little piece of my desires.   14

Enter Pistol.

Gower. Why, here he comes, swelling like a turkey cock.

Fluellen. 'Tis no matter for his swellings, nor his turkey cocks. God pless you, Aunchient Pistol! You scurvy, lousy knave, God pless you!

Pistol. Ha! art thou bedlam? Dost thou thirst, base Trojan,   20
To have me fold up Parca's fatal web?

5 **scauld** scabby, scurvy. 9 **yesterday** i.e. Saint Davy's Day.
20–2 **Ha . . . leek** F prints as prose. 20 **bedlam** lunatic. **Trojan**
a dissolute fellow. 21 **fold . . . web** cut the thread of your life;
the Parcae were the Roman Fates.

Hence! I am qualmish at the smell of leek.

Fluellen. I peseech you heartily, scurvy, lousy knave, at my desires, and my requests, and my petitions, to eat, look you, this leek. Because, look you, you do not love it, nor your affections, and your appetites and your digestions doo's not agree with it, I would desire you to eat it.   28

Pistol. Not for Cadwallader and all his goats.

Fluellen. There is one goat for you. *Strikes him.* Will you be so good, scauld knave, as eat it?

Pistol. Base Trojan, thou shalt die!   32

Fluellen. You say very true, scauld knave, when God's will is. I will desire you to live in the meantime, and eat your victuals. Come, there is sauce for it. [*Strikes him.*] You call'd me yesterday mountain squire, but I will make you today a squire of low degree. I pray you fall to. If you can mock a leek, you can eat a leek.   39

Gower. Enough, captain. You have astonish'd him.

Fluellen. I say, I will make him eat some part of my leek, or I will peat his pate four days. Bite, I pray you. It is good for your green wound and your bloody coxcomb.

Pistol. Must I bite?   45

Fluellen. Yes, certainly, and out of doubt and out of question too, and ambiguities.

Pistol. By this leek, I will most horribly revenge! I eat and eat, I swear—   49

Fluellen. Eat, I pray you. Will you have some more

22 am qualmish feel sick. 29 **Cadwallader** the last of the Welsh kings. 36–7 **mountain squire** i.e. poor Welshman. 37–8 **make . . . degree** i.e. cut you down to size (the allusion is to a popular metrical romance). 40 **astonish'd** dismayed, stunned. 43 **green** fresh, raw. 44 **coxcomb** head.

sauce to your leek? There is not enough leek to swear by.

Pistol. Quiet thy cudgel. Thou dost see I eat.   53

Fluellen. Much good do you, scauld knave, heartily. Nay, pray you throw none away. The skin is good for your broken coxcomb. When you take occasions to see leeks hereafter, I pray you mock at 'em, that is all.

Pistol. Good.   59

Fluellen. Ay, leeks is good. Hold you, there is a groat to heal your pate.

Pistol. Me a groat!

Fluellen. Yes, verily, and in truth you shall take it, or I have another leek in my pocket, which you shall eat.   65

Pistol. I take thy groat in earnest of revenge.

Fluellen. If I owe you anything, I will pay you in cudgels. You shall be a woodmonger, and buy nothing of me but cudgels. God bye you, and keep you, and heal your pate.   *Exit.*

Pistol. All hell shall stir for this!   71

Gower. Go, go. You are a counterfeit cowardly knave. Will you mock at an ancient tradition, begun upon an honorable respect and worn as a memorable trophy of predeceased valor, and dare not avouch in your deeds any of your words? I have seen you gleeking and galling at this gentleman twice or thrice. You thought because he could not speak English in the native garb he could not therefore handle an

54 **do** may it do. 59 **Good** very well. 61 **groat** fourpence. 66 **in earnest** as payment on account. 68 **woodmonger** dealer in wood. 69 **bye** be with; F *bu'y.* 73 **begun** F *began.* 74 **upon . . . respect** for an honourable reason. **memorable** commemorative. 75 **predeceased** long since dead. **avouch** support. 76-7 **gleeking** mocking. 77 **galling** annoying, scoffing. 79 **garb** fashion.

English cudgel. You find it otherwise, and henceforth
let a Welsh correction teach you a good English
condition. Fare ye well.   *Exit.*

Pistol. Doth Fortune play the huswife with me now?
News have I that my Doll is dead i' th' spital
Of malady of France,   85
And there my rendezvous is quite cut off.
Old I do wax, and from my weary limbs
Honor is cudgel'd. Well, bawd I'll turn
And something lean to cutpurse of quick hand.
To England will I steal, and there I'll steal.   90
And patches will I get unto these cudgel'd scars
And swear I got them in the Gallia wars.   *Exit.*

SCENE 2

*Enter, at one door, King Henry, Exeter, Bedford,
[Gloucester,] Warwick, [Westmoreland,] and other
Lords; at another, Queen Isabel, the [French] King,
[the Princess Katharine, Alice, and other Ladies;]
the Duke of Burgundy, and other French.*

King Henry. Peace to this meeting, wherefore we
        are met!
Unto our brother France, and to our sister,
Health and fair time of day. Joy and good wishes
To our most fair and princely cousin Katharine.

82 condition disposition, character. 83-90 Doth . . . steal F
prints as prose. 83-92 Doth . . . wars N. 83 huswife hussy, i.e.
jilt; probably pronounced 'hussif.' 84 spital hospital. 85 Of malady
of France venereal disease; F *of a.* 88 bawd pander. 89 something
. . . to to some extent turn to. 90 steal N. 92 swear F *swore.*
SD Burgundy F *Bourgongne.* 1 wherefore for which.

And as a branch and member of this royalty,   5
By whom this great assembly is contriv'd,
We do salute you, Duke of Burgundy.
And, princes French, and peers, health to you all!
  France. Right joyous are we to behold your face,
Most worthy brother England, fairly met.   10
So are you, princes English, every one.
  Queen. So happy be the issue, brother England,
Of this good day and of this gracious meeting
As we are now glad to behold your eyes—
Your eyes which hitherto have borne in them   15
Against the French, that met them in their bent,
The fatal balls of murthering basilisks.
The venom of such looks, we fairly hope,
Have lost their quality, and that this day
Shall change all griefs and quarrels into love.   20
  King Henry. To cry amen to that, thus we appear.
  Queen. You English princes all, I do salute you.
  Burgundy. My duty to you both, on equal love,
Great Kings of France and England! That I have
    labor'd   24
With all my wits, my pains, and strong endeavors
To bring your most imperial majesties
Unto this bar and royal interview,
Your mightiness on both parts best can witness.
Since then my office hath so far prevail'd
That face to face and royal eye to eye   30
You have congreeted, let it not disgrace me

5 royalty royal family. 6 contriv'd arranged. 9 France the French
king; F indicates Henry (below) by *England.* 12 England F2; F
Ireland. 16 bent gaze, line of sight or fire. 17 balls . . . basilisks
N. 19 quality essential nature. and that and (we hope) that.
20 griefs grievances. 27 bar court of decision. 31 congreeted
greeted each other.

If I demand before this royal view
What rub or what impediment there is
Why that the naked, poor, and mangled Peace,
Dear nurse of arts, plenties, and joyful births,   35
Should not in this best garden of the world,
Our fertile France, put up her lovely visage?
Alas, she hath from France too long been chas'd,
And all her husbandry doth lie on heaps,
Corrupting in it own fertility.   40
Her vine, the merry cheerer of the heart,
Unpruned dies. Her hedges even-pleach'd,
Like prisoners wildly overgrown with hair,
Put forth disorder'd twigs. Her fallow leas
The darnel, hemlock, and rank fumitory   45
Doth root upon, while that the colter rusts
That should deracinate such savagery.
The even mead, that erst brought sweetly forth
The freckled cowslip, burnet, and green clover,
Wanting the scythe, all uncorrected, rank,   50
Conceives by idleness, and nothing teems
But hateful docks, rough thistles, kecksies, burrs,
Losing both beauty and utility.
And as our vineyards, fallows, meads, and hedges,
Defective in their natures, grow to wildness,   55

32 view presence. 33 rub impediment. 36 best garden N. 37 put
up raise. 40 it its. 42 even-pleach'd evenly interwoven. 44 fallow
leas uncultivated meadows, arable land. 45 darnel . . . fumitory weeds; F *Femetary*. 46 while that while. colter blade of the
plowshare; F *Culter*. 47 deracinate uproot. 48 even mead level
meadow. erst formally. 49 burnet a weed (or herb). 50 all F
withall. 51 Conceives by is fertilized by. nothing teems brings
forth nothing. 52 docks weeds. kecksies dry stalks of the hemlock variety. 54 as F *all*. fallows plowed fields. 55 Defective . . .
natures losing or deficient in their true natures.

Even so our houses and ourselves and children
Have lost, or do not learn for want of time,
The sciences that should become our country,
But grow like savages—as soldiers will
That nothing do but meditate on blood—   60
To swearing and stern looks, defus'd attire,
And everything that seems unnatural.
Which to reduce into our former favor
You are assembled. And my speech entreats
That I may know the let why gentle Peace   65
Should not expel these inconveniences
And bless us with her former qualities.
    King Henry. If, Duke of Burgundy, you would the
        peace
Whose want gives growth to th' imperfections
Which you have cited, you must buy that peace   70
With full accord to all our just demands,
Whose tenors and particular effects
You have, enschedul'd briefly, in your hands.
    Burgundy. The king hath heard them, to the which
        as yet
There is no answer made.
    King Henry.   Well then, the peace   75
Which you before so urg'd lies in his answer.
    France. I have but with a cursitory eye
O'erglanc'd the articles. Pleaseth your grace
To appoint some of your council presently
To sit with us once more, with better heed   80

61 **defus'd** disordered, diffused. 63 **reduce** bring back. **favor** good
appearance. 65 **let** hindrance. 66 **inconveniences** misfortunes.
68 **would** desire. 69 **imperfections** five syllables. 72 **tenors** pur-
port; F *Tenures*. 73 **enschedul'd** drawn up in writing. 77 **cursitory**
(Wilson), 'cursory'; F *curselarie*; Q *cursenary*; most editors read
cursorary (Q3). 78 **Pleaseth** if it pleases. 79 **presently** at once.

To resurvey them, we will suddenly
Pass our accept and peremptory answer.

King Henry. Brother, we shall. Go, uncle Exeter,
And brother Clarence, and you, brother Gloucester,
Warwick, and Huntingdon, go with the king. 85
And take with you free power to ratify,
Augment, or alter, as your wisdoms best
Shall see advantageable for our dignity,
Anything in or out of our demands,
And we'll consign thereto. Will you, fair sister, 90
Go with the princes or stay here with us?

Queen. Our gracious brother, I will go with them.
Happily a woman's voice may do some good
When articles too nicely urg'd be stood on.

King Henry. Yet leave our cousin Katharine here
    with us. 95
She is our capital demand, compris'd
Within the forerank of our articles.

Queen. She hath good leave.

> *Exeunt. Manent King [Henry] and Katharine
> [and Alice].*

King Henry.   Fair Katharine, and most fair,
Will you vouchsafe to teach a soldier terms
Such as will enter at a lady's ear 100
And plead his love suit to her gentle heart?

Katharine. Your majesty shall mock at me. I cannot speak your England.

King Henry. O fair Katharine, if you will love me
soundly with your French heart, I will be glad to

81 **suddenly** immediately. 82 **Pass** give, pronounce. **accept** 'acceptance' or 'accepted.' **peremptory** final. 88 **advantageable** advantageous. 90 **consign** formally agree. 93 **Happily** perhaps, haply. 94 **nicely** precisely. **stood** insisted. 96 **capital** chief. 98 Exeunt F *Exeunt omnes.* 99 **terms** phrases. 101 **love suit** see Appendix B.

hear you confess it brokenly with your English
tongue. Do you like me, Kate?

Katharine. Pardonnez-moi, I cannot tell vat is 'like
me.'   109

King Henry. An angel is like you, Kate, and you
are like an angel.

Katharine. Que dit-il? Que je suis semblable à les
anges?

Alice. Oui, vraiment, sauf votre grâce, ainsi dit-il.

King Henry. I said so, dear Katharine, and I must
not blush to affirm it.   116

Katharine. O bon Dieu! Les langues des hommes
sont pleines de tromperies.

King Henry. What says she, fair one? That the
tongues of men are full of deceits?   120

Alice. Oui, dat de tongues of de mans is be full of
deceits. Dat is de princess.

King. The princess is the better Englishwoman. I'
faith, Kate, my wooing is fit for thy understanding.
I am glad thou canst speak no better English, for if
thou couldst, thou wouldst find me such a plain king
that thou wouldst think I had sold my farm to buy
my crown. I know no ways to mince it in love, but
directly to say 'I love you.' Then if you urge me
farther than to say 'Do you in faith?' I wear out my
suit. Give me your answer, i' faith, do, and so clap
hands and a bargain. How say you, lady?   132

Katharine. Sauf votre honneur, me understand vell.

King Henry. Marry, if you would put me to verses,
or to dance for your sake, Kate, why, you undid me.

108 vat F *wat* throughout; see also *vell* (F *well*), l. 133. 112–4
Que . . . dit-il What does he say? That I am like the angels?
Alice. Yes, truly, saving your grace, he says so. 128 **mince it**
speak affectedly. 130–1 **wear . . . suit** exhaust my petition
(quibble). 131 **clap** clasp. 135 **undid** would undo.

For the one I have neither words nor measure, and for the other I have no strength in measure, yet a reasonable measure in strength. If I could win a lady at leapfrog, or by vawting into my saddle with my armor on my back, under the correction of bragging be it spoken, I should quickly leap into a wife. Or if I might buffet for my love, or bound my horse for her favors, I could lay on like a butcher and sit like a jackanapes, never off. But before God, Kate, I cannot look greenly nor gasp out my eloquence, nor I have no cunning in protestation—only downright oaths, which I never use till urg'd, nor never break for urging. If thou canst love a fellow of this temper, Kate, whose face is not worth sunburning, that never looks in his glass for love of anything he sees there, let thine eye be thy cook. I speak to thee plain soldier. If thou canst love me for this, take me. If not, to say to thee that I shall die, is true—but for thy love, by the Lord, no. Yet I love thee too. And while thou liv'st, dear Kate, take a fellow of plain and uncoined constancy, for he perforce must do thee right, because he hath not the gift to woo in other places. For these fellows of infinite tongue that can rhyme themselves into ladies' favors, they do always reason themselves out again. What! A speaker is but

136-8 measure . . . measure triple pun: 'meter' . . . 'stately court dance' . . . 'amount.' 139 vawting vaulting N. 140 under . . . of subject to correction for. 142 buffet box. bound my horse make my horse prance. 144 jackanapes monkey. 145 greenly foolishly. 146 cunning skill. protestation protesting (his love). 148 temper disposition. 149 not . . . sunburning i.e. already as brown as possible. 151 let . . . cook let your eye dress this plain dish as it wishes. 156 uncoined genuine; not minted nor passing current.

a prater, a rhyme is but a ballad. A good leg will
fall, a straight back will stoop, a black beard will
turn white, a curl'd pate will grow bald, a fair face
will wither, a full eye will wax hollow. But a good
heart, Kate, is the sun and the moon, or rather the
sun and not the moon, for it shines bright and never
changes, but keeps his course truly. If thou would
have such a one, take me. And take me, take a soldier; take a soldier, take a king. And what say'st
thou then to my love? Speak, my fair, and fairly, I
pray thee.   171

Katharine. Is it possible dat I sould love de enemy
of France?

King Henry. No, it is not possible you should love
the enemy of France, Kate. But in loving me you
should love the friend of France, for I love France
so well that I will not part with a village of it. I will
have it all mine. And, Kate, when France is mine and
I am yours, then yours is France and you are mine.

Katharine. I cannot tell vat is dat.   180

King Henry. No, Kate? I will tell thee in French,
which I am sure will hang upon my tongue like a
new-married wife about her husband's neck, hardly
to be shook off. Je quand sur le possession de France,
et quand vous avez le possession de moi—let me see,
what then? Saint Denis be my speed!—donc votre
est France, et vous êtes mienne. It is as easy for me,
Kate, to conquer the kingdom as to speak so much
more French. I shall never move thee in French, unless it be to laugh at me.   190

161 **ballad** doggerel. 162 **fall** shrink. 167 **his** its. 184–7 **Je . . .
mienne** When I [have] possession of France, and when you have
possession of me . . . then France is yours and you are mine.
186 **Saint Denis** patron saint of France.

Katharine. Sauf votre honneur, le français que vous parlez, il est meilleur que l'anglais lequel je parle.

King Henry. No, faith, is't not, Kate. But thy speaking of my tongue, and I thine, most truly-falsely, must needs be granted to be much at one. But, Kate, dost thou understand thus much English? Canst thou love me?

Katharine. I cannot tell. 198

King Henry. Can any of your neighbors tell, Kate? I'll ask them. Come, I know thou lovest me, and at night, when you come into your closet, you'll question this gentlewoman about me. And I know, Kate, you will to her dispraise those parts in me that you love with your heart. But, good Kate, mock me mercifully, the rather, gentle princess, because I love thee cruelly. If ever thou beest mine, Kate, as I have a saving faith within me tells me thou shalt, I get thee with scambling, and thou must therefore needs prove a good soldier-breeder. Shall not thou and I, between Saint Denis and Saint George, compound a boy, half French, half English, that shall go to Constantinople and take the Turk by the beard? Shall we not? What say'st thou, my fair flower-de-luce?

Katharine. I do not know dat. 214

King Henry. No, 'tis hereafter to know, but now to promise. Do but now promise, Kate, you will endeavor for your French part of such a boy, and for my English moiety take the word of a king and a

191–2 Sauf . . . parle Saving your honor, the French that you speak is better than the English that I speak. 195 at one alike. 201 closet private apartment. 208 with scambling by scuffling, fighting. 212 the Turk the Grand Turk, the Sultan. 213 flower-de-luce *fleur-de-lis*, the emblem of France. 218 moiety share.

bachelor. How answer you, la plus belle Katharine
du monde, mon très cher et divin déesse?   220

Katharine. Your majestee 'ave fausse French
enough to deceive de most sage damoiselle dat is en
France.   223

King Henry. Now, fie upon my false French! By
mine honor, in true English, I love thee, Kate; by
which honor I dare not swear thou lovest me. Yet my
blood begins to flatter me that thou dost, notwith-
standing the poor and untempering effect of my
visage. Now beshrew my father's ambition! He was
thinking of civil wars when he got me; therefore was
I created with a stubborn outside, with an aspect of
iron, that when I come to woo ladies, I fright them.
But in faith, Kate, the elder I wax, the better I shall
appear. My comfort is that old age, that ill layer-up
of beauty, can do no more spoil upon my face. Thou
hast me, if thou hast me, at the worst, and thou
shalt wear me, if thou wear me, better and better.
And therefore tell me, most fair Katharine, will you
have me? Put off your maiden blushes, avouch the
thoughts of your heart with the looks of an empress,
take me by the hand, and say 'Harry of England, I
am thine.' Which word thou shalt no sooner bless
mine ear withal but I will tell thee aloud 'England
is thine, Ireland is thine, France is thine, and Henry
Plantagenet is thine'—who, though I speak it before
his face, if he be not fellow with the best king, thou
shalt find the best king of good fellows. Come, your

219 **bachelor** young knight. 219–20 **la plus . . . déesse** the most
beautiful Katharine in the world, my very dear and divine goddess. 227 **blood** natural impulse. 228 **untempering** unsoftening,
unattractive. 229 **beshrew** confound. 230 **got** begot. 231 **stubborn**
rude, rough. 239 **avouch** declare.

answer in broken music, for thy voice is music, and
thy English broken. Therefore, queen of all, Katharine, break thy mind to me in broken English. Wilt
thou have me? 251

Katharine. Dat is as it sall please de roi mon père.

King Henry. Nay, it will please him well, Kate. It
shall please him, Kate.

Katharine. Den it sall also content me. 255

King Henry. Upon that I kiss your hand, and I
call you my queen.

Katharine. Laissez, mon seigneur, laissez, laissez!
Ma foi, je ne veux point que vous abaissiez votre
grandeur en baisant la main d'une de votre seigneurie
indigne serviteur. Excusez-moi, je vous supplie, mon
très-puissant seigneur. 262

King Henry. Then I will kiss your lips, Kate.

Katharine. Les dames et damoiselles pour être
baisées devant leur noces, il n'est pas la coutume de
France. 266

King Henry. Madam my interpreter, what says she?

Alice. Dat it is not be de fashon pour les ladies of
France—I cannot tell vat is 'baiser' en Anglish.

King Henry. To kiss. 270

Alice. Your majestee entendre bettre que moi.

King Henry. It is not a fashion for the maids in
France to kiss before they are married, would she
say?

248 **broken music** garbled English; music arranged for parts.
250 **break** reveal. 252 **roi mon père** king my father. 258–62
Laissez . . . seigneur Don't, my lord, don't, don't! I do not
wish you to lower your greatness by kissing the hand of your
unworthy servant. Excuse me, I beg you, my most powerful
lord. 264–6 **Les dames . . . France** For ladies and young girls
to be kissed before their marriage—it is not the custom in France.
271 **Your . . . moi** Your majesty understands better than I.

132

Alice. Oui, vraiment.   275

King Henry. O Kate, nice customs cursy to great
kings. Dear Kate, you and I cannot be confin'd
within the weak list of a country's fashion. We are
the makers of manners, Kate, and the liberty that
follows our places stops the mouth of all find-faults,
as I will do yours for upholding the nice fashion of
your country in denying me a kiss. Therefore, patiently and yielding. [*Kisses her.*] You have witch-
craft in your lips, Kate. There is more eloquence in
a sugar touch of them than in the tongues of the
French council, and they should sooner persuade
Harry of England than a general petition of monarchs. Here comes your father.

*Enter the French Power, [the French King and
Queen, Burgundy,] and the English Lords.*

Burgundy. God save your majesty! My royal
cousin, teach you our princess English?   290

King Henry. I would have her learn, my fair cousin,
how perfectly I love her, and that is good English.

Burgundy. Is she not apt?

King Henry. Our tongue is rough, coz, and my condition is not smooth; so that, having neither the
voice nor the heart of flattery about me, I cannot
so conjure up the spirit of love in her that he will
appear in his true likeness.   298

Burgundy. Pardon the frankness of my mirth if I
answer you for that. If you would conjure in her,
you must make a circle; if conjure up love in her in
his true likeness, he must appear naked and blind.

275 **Oui, vraiment** Yes, truly. 276 **nice** fastidious. **cursy** curtsy,
bow. 278 **list** boundary. 280 **follows . . . places** goes with our
position. 294–5 **condition** disposition.

Can you blame her, then, being a maid yet ros'd over with the virgin crimson of modesty, if she deny the appearance of a naked blind boy in her naked seeing self? It were, my lord, a hard condition for a maid to consign to.

King Henry. Yet they do wink and yield, as love is blind and enforces.

Burgundy. They are then excus'd, my lord, when they see not what they do.   311

King Henry. Then, good my lord, teach your cousin to consent winking.

Burgundy. I will wink on her to consent, my lord, if you will teach her to know my meaning. For maids well summer'd and warm kept are like flies at Bartholomewtide, blind, though they have their eyes. And then they will endure handling, which before would not abide looking on.   319

King Henry. This moral ties me over to time and a hot summer. And so I shall catch the fly, your cousin, in the latter end, and she must be blind too.

Burgundy. As love is, my lord, before it loves.

King Henry. It is so. And you may, some of you, thank love for my blindness, who cannot see many a fair French city for one fair French maid that stands in my way.   327

French King. Yes, my lord, you see them perspectively—the cities turn'd into a maid, for they are all girdled with maiden walls that war hath never ent'red.   331

308 **wink** shut the eyes. 316 **summer'd** nurtured. 316–7 **flies** . . . **Bartholomewtide** i.e. August 24, when flies are torpid in the late summer. 320 **This moral** i.e. the moral to be drawn from this. 328–9 **perspectively** as though seen through a 'perspective,' a glass which produces optical illusions. 330 **never** not in F.

134

King Henry. Shall Kate be my wife?

French King. So please you.

King Henry. I am content, so the maiden cities you talk of may wait on her. So the maid that stood in the way for my wish shall show me the way to my will.

French King. We have consented to all terms of reason.

King Henry. Is't so, my lords of England? 340

Westmoreland. The king hath granted every article: His daughter first, and then in sequel all, According to their firm proposed natures.

Exeter. Only he hath not yet subscribed this: Where your majesty demands that the King of France, having any occasion to write for matter of grant, shall name your highness in this form and with this addition, in French, 'Notre très-cher fils Henri, Roi d'Angleterre, Héritier de France'; and thus in Latin, 'Praeclarissimus filius noster Henricus, Rex Angliae et Haeres Franciae.' 351

French King. Nor this I have not, brother, so denied,
But your request shall make me let it pass.

King Henry. I pray you, then, in love and dear alliance,
Let that one article rank with the rest, 355
And thereupon give me your daughter.

French King. Take her, fair son, and from her blood raise up

334 so *so long as.* 335 wait on *accompany (as dowry).* 337 will desire. 342 then F2; F *and in sequele.* 343 firm . . . natures *the definite character of the terms proposed.* 344 subscribed *signed, assented to.* Where *whereas.* 346 matter of grant *i.e. documents conferring lands or titles.* 347–8 addition *title.* 350 Praeclarissimus *most renowned N.*

Issue to me, that the contending kingdoms
Of France and England, whose very shores look pale
With envy of each other's happiness,   360
May cease their hatred, and this dear conjunction
Plant neighborhood and Christianlike accord
In their sweet bosoms, that never war advance
His bleeding sword 'twixt England and fair France.
  Lords. Amen!   365
  King Henry. Now welcome, Kate. And bear me wit-
    ness all
That here I kiss her as my sovereign queen. *Flourish.*
  Queen. God, the best maker of all marriages,
Combine your hearts in one, your realms in one!
As man and wife, being two, are one in love,   370
So be there 'twixt your kingdoms such a spousal
That never may ill office or fell jealousy,
Which troubles oft the bed of blessed marriage,
Thrust in between the paction of these kingdoms
To make divorce of their incorporate league;   375
That English may as French, French Englishmen,
Receive each other. God speak this Amen!
  All. Amen!
  King Henry. Prepare we for our marriage, on which
    day,
My Lord of Burgundy, we'll take your oath   380
And all the peers', for surety of our leagues.
Then shall I swear to Kate, and you to me,
And may our oaths well kept and prosp'rous be!
                                Sennet. Exeunt.

361 **conjunction** union. 371 **spousal** marriage. 372 **ill office** any
hostile act. 374 **paction** alliance; F *Pation.* 381 **surety** ratification.
383 **Sennet** set of notes on a trumpet.

[Epilogue]

Enter Chorus.

Thus far, with rough and all-unable pen,
Our bending author hath pursu'd the story,
In little room confining mighty men,
Mangling by starts the full course of their glory.
Small time, but in that small most greatly liv'd   5
This star of England. Fortune made his sword,
By which the world's best garden he achiev'd,
And of it left his son imperial lord.
Henry the Sixth, in infant bands crown'd King
Of France and England, did this king succeed,   10
Whose state so many had the managing
That they lost France and made his England bleed.
Which oft our stage hath shown, and for their sake
In your fair minds let this acceptance take. [Exit.]

SD **Epilogue** a sonnet. 2 **bending** i.e. under the weight of his task;
bowing. 4 **Mangling by starts** marring by telling it in fits and
starts. 7 **achiev'd** won. 9 **infant bands** swaddling clothes. 13
oft . . . shown clear proof of the popularity of the three parts
of *King Henry VI.* 14 **let . . . take** may this receive your favor.

NOTES

The Actors' Names *King Henry the Fifth:* born 1387, became king 1413, died 1422; eldest son of Henry IV. His campaigns in France and his marriage to Princess Katharine mark the high point of Lancastrian rule in England.

Duke of Gloucester (1391–1447): Humphrey, youngest son of Henry IV and possibly the only one of Henry's brothers actually present at Agincourt; after Henry's death deputy-protector of England; patron of Lydgate (see 2 *Henry IV* and 1, 2 *Henry VI*).

Duke of Bedford (1389–1435): John of Lancaster, third son of Henry IV; left in England as lieutenant of the kingdom during the Agincourt campaign; later regent of France and protector of England under Henry VI; famous for his role in the burning of Joan of Arc (see 1, 2 *Henry IV* and 1 *Henry VI*).

Duke of Exeter: Thomas Beaufort, youngest son of John of Gaunt by Catherine Swynford; probably left by Henry in command at Harfleur, though in Shakespeare's sources Exeter leaves Sir John Fastolfe at Harfleur and rejoins the king (see 1 *Henry VI*).

Duke of York: son of Edmund, fifth son of Edward III; called 'Aumerle' in *Richard II*. After his death at Agincourt his title passed to the son of his brother Richard, Earl of Cambridge (see below). This son's claim to the throne in the next reign initiated the wars of York and Lancaster.

Earl of Salisbury: Thomas Montacute; slain at the siege of Orleans, 1428 (see 1 *Henry VI*).

Earl of Westmoreland: Ralph Neville, Warden of the Scotch Marches; supporter of Bolingbroke against Richard II (see 1, 2 *Henry IV*).

Earl of Warwick: a governor of the young king Henry VI (see 2 *Henry IV* and 1, 2 *Henry VI*).

Archbishop of Canterbury: Henry Chichele, founder of All Soul's College, Oxford; an opponent of Wycliffe and a warm advocate of the war in France.

Bishop of Ely: John Fordham, once the secretary of Richard II.

Earl of Cambridge: Richard, second son of Edmund, Duke of York (see *Richard II*); executed in 1415 for plotting to put the

Earl of March on the throne; father of Richard, Duke of York (slain at Wakefield in 1460), whose youngest son became Richard III.

Lord Scroop: eldest son of Sir Stephen Scroop (see *Richard II*) and nephew of the Archbishop in the *Henry IV* plays; beheaded 1415.

Sir Thomas Grey: son-in-law of the Earl of Westmoreland; executed 1415.

Sir Thomas Erpingham: steward of the king's house; mentioned in Drayton's 'Ballad of Agincourt' as commander of the English archers.

Charles the Sixth, King of France: born 1368, became king 1380, died 1422. Since he survived Henry by two months, Henry never became King of France. His eldest daughter, Isabella, was the second queen of Richard II, and his youngest, Katharine the Fair, appears in this play. He was subject to prolonged fits of insanity and was present neither at Agincourt nor at Troyes, at the betrothal of his daughter.

Lewis, the Dauphin: His brother became Charles VII, who died in 1461. Actually there were three Dauphins during the period of this play.

Duke of Burgundy: in III.5.42 and IV.8.96 John the Fearless; in V.2 Philip the Good. After the murder of his father by adherents of the Dauphin Charles, Philip brought about the peace between Charles VI and Henry V, thus excluding the Dauphin from the succession.

Duke of Orleans: imprisoned in England for twenty-five years after Agincourt, where he wrote some of the finest French poetry of the century.

The Constable of France: Charles de la Bret, half-brother of Henry V; commanded the French army at Agincourt and was killed there.

Isabel, Queen of France: daughter of Stephen II of Bavaria. Unable to control the two parties fighting for power in France, led by the Duke of Burgundy and the Duke of Orleans (the Armagnacs), she consented to the treaty of Troyes, in which Henry V became heir to the French throne.

Katharine: married Henry V in 1420 and became the mother of Henry VI; by her second husband, Owen Tudor, grandmother of Henry VII of England.

Prologue

1SD **Prologue** This is a single figure, the 'chorus' of the play, who speaks a prologue before each of the acts. Nowhere else does Shakespeare employ the chorus so consistently as in this play.

9 **spirits . . . hath** Shakespeare frequently employs singular forms of verbs with plural subjects.

11 **cockpit** The round or octagonal theater was similar to the pits in which cockfights were held.

13 **wooden O** Probably the Curtain (rather than the Globe) theater, where the play was performed.

15 **crooked figure** Curved, like a naught, which in the unit's place and along with other figures may represent a million.

Act I, Scene 1

7–19 **It must . . . the bill** The following passage from Shakespeare's principal source, Holinshed's *Chronicles* (see Appendix B), suggests the detailed nature of his borrowing. Shakespeare underplays (ll. 7–8, 75–81) the clergy's motive for wanting war. The bill recommended

> that the temporall lands deuoutlie giuen, and disordinatlie spent by religious, and other spirituall persons, should be seized into the kings hands, sith the same might suffice to mainteine, to the honor of the king, and defense of the realme, fifteene earles, fifteene hundred knights, six thousand and two hundred esquiers, and a hundred almessehouses, for reliefe onelie of the poore, impotent, and needie persons, and the king to haue cleerelie to his coffers twentie thousand pounds, with manie other prouisions and values of religious houses, which I passe ouer.

140

> This bill was much noted, and more feared among the
> religious sort, whom suerlie it touched verie neere, and there-
> fore to find remedie against it, they determined to assaie
> all waies to put by and ouerthrow this bill: wherein they
> thought best to trie if they might mooue the kings mood
> with some sharpe inuention, that he should not regard the
> importunate petitions of the commons.

On his deathbed, Henry's father had advised his son to 'busy
giddy minds With foreign quarrels' (2 *Henry IV*, IV.5.214–15),
in order to lessen the civil strife that had so shaken the previous
reign. Shakespeare does not mention this reason for war in the
next scene, nor does he render it easy for us to decide to what
degree this king is like the 'politician,' his father. See the two
long interviews between Henry IV and Prince Hal (1 *Henry IV*,
III.2 and 2 *Henry IV*, IV.5).

16 **corporal** As in rapid modern speech, the following three-
syllable words (among others) probably had the value of dissylla-
bles: *opening* (I.2.16), *reverence* (I.2.20), *pilfering* (I.2.142),
prisoner (I.2.162), *natural* (I.2.182 and II.2.107), *barbarous*
(I.2.271), *treacherous* (II.Pro.22), *Covering* (II.4.38), *reverend*
(III.3.37), and so on. Similarly *You would* in l. 42 is probably
'You'd.'

17 **supplied** To prevent misreading, this text does not indicate
elision in *ied* endings, e.g. *mortified* and *satisfied*.

24 **courses . . . youth** In the two parts of *Henry IV*, the young
prince is a drinking companion of Falstaff and the despair of his
father the king. (See II.4.137 N.)

29 **offending Adam** This allusion to original sin, to sinfulness
inherited from Adam, parallels closely the baptismal service from
the *Book of Common Prayer*. Compare also Genesis 3:23–4.

33 **flood** Probably an allusion to Hercules' cleansing of the
Augean stables by turning a river through them.

89 **Edward** Edward III of England, son of Isabella, the daughter of Philip IV of France. When Isabella, after the death of her
brothers, claimed the throne of France for her son Edward, an
assembly of French peers and barons barred inheritance through
the female.

Act I, Scene 2

11 law Salic The Salic law forbade the succession of a woman to the French throne, as Canterbury explains below. (See I.1.89 N.)

27–8 gives . . . makes Another instance of the apparent lack of agreement between subject and verb. Compare *is . . . wretches*, l. 243.

46 Charles the Great Ll. 35–100 are taken almost line by line from Holinshed. For closeness to the source they are probably unique in Shakespeare. The dates of the reigns of the sovereigns mentioned, in chronological order, are as follows: Clothair I, 558–61; Childeric III, 742–51 (last of the Merovingian kings, deposed by Pepin); Pepin, 752–68 (son of Charles Martel and founder of the Carlovingian dynasty); Charles the Great (Charlemagne), 768–814 (son of Pepin); Louis I, *le Débonnaire*, 814–40 (son of Charlemagne); Charles I, the Bald (called Charlemagne, l. 75), 840–77; Hugh Capet, 987–96 (defeated Charles, Duke of Lorraine; was elected to the throne after the death of Louis V, and founded the dynasty which bears his name); Louis IX (called Lewis the Tenth, l. 77), 1226–70, Saint Louis.

77 Lewis the Tenth Actually Louis IX. Throughout this passage, as elsewhere in the play, Shakespeare is following Holinshed's *Chronicles* so closely that he reproduces entire phrases and several of Holinshed's errors.

86–102 So that . . . ancestors Compare simile, proper names, and phrasing (see l. 131 below) with the following passage from Holinshed:

> . . . so that more cleere than the sunne it openlie appeareth, that the title of king Pepin, the claime of Hugh Capet, the possession of Lewes, yea and the French kings to this daie, are deriued and conueied from the heire female, though they would vnder the colour of such a fained law, barre the kings and princes of this realme of England of their right and lawfull inheritance.
>
> The archbishop further alledged out of the booke of Numbers this saieng: When a man dieth without a sonne, let the inheritance descend to his daughter. At length, hauing said

142

sufficientlie for the proofe of the kings iust and lawfull title
to the crowne of France, he exhorted him to aduance foorth
his banner to fight for his right, to conquer his inheritance,
to spare neither bloud, sword, nor fire, sith his warre was
iust, his cause good, and his claime true.

94 amply to imbare Many editors follow *imbar* (F3), a variant
of 'embar,' interpreting it variously to mean 'bar in,' 'secure,'
'exclude,' etc. The form *imbar* may be supported by the three
occurrences of the word *bar* in the Archbishop's speech (Walter).
F reads *imbarre*.

173 tame Many editors read *tear* (after Rowe); Q *spoyle*.

187 honeybees This was a familiar parallel in Shakespeare's
day and is found among other places in Lyly's *Euphues*.

221 Dolphin The heir apparent to the French throne. The F
spelling is retained throughout.

232 Turkish mute A slave whose tongue is removed to prevent
his betraying royal secrets.

258–66 Tennis . . . chases This extended figure (and ll. 250–3
above) is derived from Holinshed. The ambassadors

> . . . brought with them a barrell of Paris balles, which from
> their maister they presented to him for a token that was
> taken in verie ill part, as sent in scorne, to signifie, that it
> was more meet for the king to passe the time with such
> childish exercise, than to attempt any worthie exploit. Wher-
> fore the K. wrote to him, that yer ought long, he would
> tosse him some London balles that perchance should shake
> the walles of the best court in France.

262–6 set . . . chases These are terms from the popular court
tennis of the day: *hazard*, places from which the ball cannot be
returned; *wrangler*, opponent; *chases*, second bounds of the ball,
a missed return.

Act II, Prologue

1SD Flourish Act II is not indicated here in F. Act III is
marked *Secundus* and Act IV *Tertius*. The F *Flourish* here and
at the entry of the chorus before Act III possibly belongs with
the final lines of Acts I and II.

7 winged . . . Mercuries The herald and messenger of the gods, Mercury or Hermes, is represented as wearing winged sandals and a winged cap.

39-40 For . . . play The original Prologue may have ended with this couplet. Ll. 41-2 may prepare for the later addition of scenes 1 and 3. (See Appendix A.)

Act II, Scene 1

19 Nell Quickly Hostess of Falstaff's favorite tavern, the Boar's Head, in Eastcheap. In *Quickly*, *-ly* rhymes with 'lie.'

24-5 Though . . . plod 'To be patient is fatiguing, but it will achieve its object in the end.' F reads 'may, though . . . plodde, there.' Many sentences in the prose of F are separated only by commas.

30 tyke All of Pistol's following speeches (except ll. 62-4) are printed as prose in F.

54 Pistol's cock The 16th-century pistol was a small, noisy, inaccurate weapon. A *pistólfo* was a rogue who lived by his wits.

61 humor *Humor* could mean anything from 'temperament' to 'whim.' Through Nym's repetitions of this word and other phrases, Shakespeare seems to be parodying their excessive use in his day.

76-9 No . . . espouse Doll is Falstaff's girl in 2 *Henry IV*, and the Hostess once disliked her present husband. These are possible signs that this scene and II.3 were added later. (See II.3.10 N.) A 'tear sheet' was a sheet of high quality (quibble).

78 lazar . . . kind Cressida, proverbial after (though not in) Chaucer as a prostitute, was frequently referred to in such terms as *lazar* (beggar, leper) and *kite* (a bird of prey) or *kit* (Kate, a loose woman). Doll was sent to prison in 2 *Henry IV*, V.4.

85-6 face . . . pan See 1 *Henry IV*, III.3.26-55, for Bardolph's fiery face.

89 kill'd his heart See the famous rejection of Falstaff in 2 *Henry IV*, V.5.48 ff.

92 divel The spellings *deuil*, *diuel*, and *deule* are used interchangeably in F.

108 noble A third of a pound (6s. 8d.), less than the eight shillings Nym asked for, because this is to be cash payment.

120 quotidian tertian The Hostess is as usual confused. The fever called the *quotidian* recurs daily, the *tertian* every other day. The Q *tashan contigian* suggests Mrs. Quickly's pronunciation.

125 fracted Pistol's flair for high-sounding terms prompts him to give such words meanings of his own. The two words here may mean 'broken and contrite' (or 'corrupted'), or 'humbled and full of grace' (Walter).

127 passes . . . careers He gives his temperament free reign. *Passes* means 'indulges in.' A *career* is a short fast gallop.

Act II, Scene 2

114–17 suggest . . . piety Tempt to damnable acts with a patchwork of arguments, to give a deceptive appearance of righteousness.

127–40 Show . . . suspicion Compare this portrait of (what Henry thought to be) a kind of ideal man with the terms in which Shakespeare characterizes Richard II's folly, Henry IV's policy, Falstaff's fatness and rioting, John of Gaunt's leanness and sense of responsibility, and the virtues of the 'mirror' of kings, Henry V.

159 sufferance This word and *heartily* here and *dangerous* in ll. 162 and 186 are probably dissyllabic. Also read 'discov'ry' in l. 162.

167–81 You have . . . hence Holinshed gives Henry's speech this form:

> Having thus conspired the death and destruction of me, which am the head of the realme and gouernour of the people, it maie be (no doubt) but that you likewise haue sworne the confusion of all that are here with me, and also the desolation of your owne countrie. To what horror (O Lord) for any true English hart to consider, that such an execrable iniquitie should euer so bewrap you, as for pleasing of a forren enemie to imbrue your hands in your bloud, and to ruine your owne natiue soile. Reuenge herein touching my person, though I seeke not; yet for the safegard of you my deere freends, & for due preseruation of all sorts, I am by office to cause example to be shewed. Get ye hence therefore ye poore miserable wretches to the receiuing of your iust

reward, wherein Gods maiestie giue you grace of his mercie
and repentance of your heinous offenses.

Act II, Scene 3

10 **A'** The frequency of the occurrence of this form of 'he'
(fourteen times) and the appearance of other characteristic
Shakespearean colloquialisms and spellings in this scene in F
(e.g. *brissle*, *vp-peer'd*, *Deules*, *rumatique*, *shogg*) suggest that the
scene (and others) may have been added in Shakespeare's hand
to an earlier manuscript of the play copied out by a scribe
(Walter; see Appendix A).

11–12 **christome** This word is probably a fusion of 'chrisom-
child' and 'christened child' (Kökeritz). Q reads *crysombd*.

17 **a' babbled . . . fields** F prints 'a Table of greene fields.'
Theobald's emendation given here is perhaps the most famous
ever made on a Shakespearean text. *Table* is probably, however,
a misprint for 'talke' (Harrison) or 'talkt' (Prouty). Q reads
'And talk of floures.'

27 **sack** Falstaff's favorite drink. See 2 *Henry IV*, IV.3.103–35.

Act II, Scene 4

25 **Whitsun . . . dance** Whitsuntide in the spring was an occasion for festivities and open-air folk dancing.

37 **Brutus** Brutus the Liberator planned to drive King Tarquin
out of Rome, while pretending to be an idiot.

54 **Cressy battle** The spelling in F of several French proper
names (*Harflew*, *Callice*, *Roan*) is retained throughout this text.

99 **fierce** This reading of F and Q may be a printer's error for
'fierie.' The word *fierce* is probably dissyllabic here.

132 **Louvre** The F *Louer* suggests pronunciation and the point
of the next line. See I.2.258–66 N.

137 **weighs time** The significance of Henry's weighing of time
should be seen in the light of the many earlier references to Prince
Hal's need to 'redeem' the time he wasted in his youth (1 *Henry
IV*, I.2.218 ff., III.2.129 ff., V.4.47 ff.; 2 *Henry IV*, II.4.390 ff.,
V.2.126 ff., etc.). See also Warwick's defense of the Prince's
idling (2 *Henry IV*, IV.4.68 ff.), partly echoed by the two bishops

in the first scene of this play. Passages which suggest the relationship between time and Richard II (*Richard II*, II.1.195 ff., V.5.45 ff., etc.), Hotspur (1 *Henry IV*, V.2.82 ff., and V.4.77 ff.), and Falstaff are especially illuminating.

140SD **Flourish** In F. This SD is transferred to the end of the scene by most editors, but the king may rise here, thus dismissing the embassy.

Act III, Scene 1

7 **summon** The new Arden edition suggests that the generally accepted *summon* is a far less likely emendation for the F *commune* than the more probable 'coniure' or 'conjure' (see V.2.297, 300, 301).

25 **yeomen** The longbowmen drawn from these freeholders were unbeatable at Crécy, Poitiers, and Agincourt.

27 **mettle . . . pasture** The F *mettell* brings both 'mettle' and 'metal' to life in this word. This play is especially rich in puns and equivocations of this kind, only a few of which can be indicated in the glosses.

Act III, Scene 2

9–12 **Knocks . . . fame** F prints these lines and ll. 16–21 and 24–7 below as prose.

23 **cullions** The strangeness of this speech in Fluellen's mouth and Pistol's replying with *great duke*, the infrequency of Fluellen's substituting *p*'s for *b*'s (only in *plow*, perhaps, l. 66), the unusual number of oaths (nine by *Cheshu* or *Chrish*, from l. 66 to l. 137), and the speech headings in F (*Welch, Scot, Irish*)—all may suggest that this independent scene is a later addition to the play. (See Appendix A.)

58 **Gloucester** Holinshed records that

> . . . the duke of Glocester, to whome the order of the siege was committed, made three mines vnder the ground, and approching to the wals with his engins and ordinance, would not suffer them within to take anie rest. For although they with their countermining somwhat disappointed the Englishmen, & came to fight with them hand to hand within the

mines, so that they went no further forward with that worke;
yet they were so inclosed on ech side, as well by water as
land, that succour they saw could none come to them.

71 Fluellen F reads *Welch*. Throughout this scene for *Jamy* F
reads *Scot*, and for Macmorris F reads *Irish*. (See III.6.1SD N.)

86 Jamy Jamy's speech gives us a good example of the Scots
employed in plays of Shakespeare's time.

Act III, Scene 3

2 latest parle This passage and a few others in the play (see
IV.6.37 N) probably prompted Yeats to say what others have said
in varying ways, that Henry 'has the gross vices, the coarse nerves,
of one who is to rule among violent people. . . . He is as re-
morseless and undistinguished as some natural force.' The king
of this scene must be viewed, however, with the Henry of the
choruses and of IV.1.

Act III, Scene 4

3 Un peu F *En peu*. The curious French of F has been clarified
and normalized by many editors. Some of the F forms, like this
one, perhaps, suggest attempts at phonetic spelling. A great
many represent older French (frequently provincial) forms: *este*
for *êtes*, *parlas* for *parles*, *doyts* for *doigts*, *escholier* for *écolier*,
dict for *dites*, *apprins* for *appris*, *vostre* for *vôtre*, *desia* for *deja*,
Anglois for *anglais*, and so on. Many other odd forms in F are
attributable to Shakespeare's handwriting and to the compositor's
ignorance of French. This scene is reproduced in full in the French
of F at the end of Appendix A.

8 Et les doigts F assigns these words to Alice, the following
speech to Katharine, and part of the next ('La main . . . écolier')
to Alice. Much of the humor of this scene derives from the sound
in French of several of the English words—*foot* (*foutre*), and *count*
(*con[t]*) for 'gown'—and from translations like *nick* (pudendum)
for 'neck' and *sin* for 'chin.'

Act III, Scene 5

1SD **Britaine** Not in F. Most editors give the Q *Burbon* here,
but the following relevant speeches are headed *Brit*. in F, and

Holinshed names Britaine, not Bourbon, as of the king's council.

9 overlook . . . grafters Shall slips (scions) taken from French stock overtop the parent trees? The Dauphin is referring to the uniting of Norman French and native Anglo-Saxon blood after 1066.

44 Faulconbridge Often given as *Fauconbridge* or *Fauconberg*. Holinshed suggests the correct forms of F *Loys* and *Lestrale* in the next line. (See IV.8.98–9.)

Act III, Scene 6

1SD English and Welsh By such tags Shakespeare points up the national characteristics of the leaders united under Henry. However, the duplication in this entry notice (*Welsh . . . Fluellen*), and the substitution in Fluellen's speeches here of *p* for *b* only once (*pridge*, l. 13) suggest possible revision of the first part of this scene. After Pistol leaves the stage at l. 61 there are ten such substitutions. (See Appendix A.) The *bridge* in l. 2 is over the little river Ternoise at Blangy. Henry and his army crossed it on October 24, 1415, the night before the battle of Agincourt.

8–9 live . . . living The first word may be an anticipation of the second, but *live* occurs at III.7.62 for 'lief' and *liveless* at IV.2.55 for 'lifeless.'

41 pax A plate stamped with a picture of Christ, the Virgin, or a saint. Holinshed mentions the stealing of a pyx, the vessel containing the consecrated wafer, by an unnamed soldier: 'Yet in this great necessitie, the poore people of the countrie were not spoiled, nor anie thing taken of them without paiment, nor anie outrage or offense doone by the Englishmen, except one, which was, that a souldiour took a pix out of a church, for which he was apprehended, & the king not once remooued till the box was restored, and the offender strangled.'

58 figo The accompanying insulting gesture is made by inserting the thumb between two closed fingers or into the mouth. The gesture is repeated with 'fig of Spain,' at l. 61.

166–8 If we . . . Discolor This phrasing is directly from Holinshed. Henry says 'If anie of your nation attempt once to stop me in my iournie now towards Calis, at their ieopardie be it;

and yet wish I not anie of you so vnaduised, as to be the occasion
that I die your tawnie ground with your red bloud.'

Act III, Scene 7

1SD **Dolphin** In III.5.64–6 the French king requests that the
Dauphin not go to battle.

13–14 **as if . . . hairs** The word may be 'hares' (F *hayres*).
This passage, like several in French in this play, is very similar
to one in John Eliot's lively English and French conversation
manual, *Ortho-epia Gallica*, 1593.

24 **jades** Many of the words in this passage have double meanings—e.g. *jade* (a term of contempt for a woman or a horse),
and *horse*-whores. (See III.4.8 N.)

67–8 **Le . . . bourbier** 'The dog is turned to his own vomit
again, and the sow that was washed to her wallowing in the mire.'
(2 Peter 2:22.)

117–18 **hooded . . . bate** 'It is never very apparent, and when
it does appear it rapidly diminishes.' The metaphor is from falconry. The hawk was carried with a hood over its head, and when
this was removed it would *bate*, i.e. flap its wings before flight.
But *bate* here also means 'abate,' 'diminish.'

156–8 **give . . . devils** The claim that Shakespeare consulted
Edward Hall's chronicle (1548) in writing this play is supported
by parallels like the following (not in Holinshed). Hall's Constable
says '. . . keepe an Englishman one moneth from his warme bed,
fat befe and stale drynke, and let him that season tast colde and
suffre hunger, you then shall se his courage abated.'

Act IV, Prologue

13 **rivets** Knights were literally riveted into parts of their
armor and could not get out without help.

43 **like the sun** See Prince Hal's comparing of himself with the
sun (1 *Henry IV*, I.2.220 ff.) and the use of sun imagery to char-
acterize Richard II.

50–2 **With . . . Agincourt** Unless Shakespeare (improbably)
is referring to Pistol and the Frenchman (IV.4) or Fluellen and
Williams (IV.8), we do not see these *foils* or this *brawl*. Perhaps
some encounter has been omitted.

Act IV, Scene 1

3 Good Though the choruses and his friends pay Henry un-qualified and convincing personal tribute from the beginning, the following scene affords us the first sustained inward view of the king as man and soldier in the play. Compare the tone of the king's speeches here with that of his soliloquies as prince (1 *Henry IV*, I.2.218 ff. and 2 *Henry IV*, IV.5.21 ff.).

12SD Erpingham The king's request to Sir Thomas to assemble the nobles at his tent is repeated twice (ll. 27 and 291), and ll. 31–2 prepare us for a soliloquy which is delayed until l. 234. Since this first soliloquy is closely related to the previous con-versation, it may have been that only the second (ll. 293–309, after Erpingham's return) appeared in a possible first form of the play. (See Appendix A.)

35 Qui va là F *Che vous la?*; Q *Ke ve la?* 'Kivala' was Eliza-bethan thieves' argot for 'Who goes there?' (See III.7.13–14 N.) F prints Pistol's speeches as prose.

71 Pompey's camp Fluellen is mistaken, for Pompey's camp before Pharsalia was notoriously undisciplined.

229–33 Indeed . . . clipper *Crowns* means both 'heads' and 'coins.' The French, outnumbering the English, *may lay* ('bet') more crowns on their victory. But it's not treason for an English-man to 'clip' (cut off) French crowns. 'Clipping' (cutting off the edges of) English crowns (coins) was punishable by death, be-cause it made them lighter and debased their value.

237–41 We must . . . enjoy F 'We . . . all./O . . . Great-nesse,/Subiect . . . sence/No . . . wringing./What . . . neg-lect,/That . . . enioy?'

249 soul of adoration F 'What? is thy Soule of Odoration?' (*adoration* has five syllables and *condition*, l. 237, has four.)

295 reck'ning, if Possibly 'reck'ning or'; F 'reckning of'; Q 'rekconing,/That . . . May not appall their courage.'

296–309 Not today . . . pardon See 2 *Henry IV*, IV.5.184–220. Henry's father was a usurper and responsible for the murder of Richard II. With this prayer, Henry seems to free England at least temporarily from the blight prophesied by the Bishop of Carlisle (*Richard II*, IV.1.114 ff.). Holinshed writes that Henry

151

'caused the bodie of king Richard to be remooued with all funerall dignitie conuenient for his estate, from Langlie to Westminster, where he was honorablie interred with queene Anne his first wife, in a solemne toome erected and set vp at the charges of this king.'

Act IV, Scene 3

11–14 **Farwell . . . valor** In F ll. 13–14 follow l. 11, and all are attributed to Bedford. Then follows l. 12, which is given to Exeter.

16–18 **O . . . today** Shakespeare heightens a passage in Holinshed:

> It is said, that as he heard one of the host vtter his wish to another thus: I would to God there were with vs now so manie good soldiers as are at this houre within England! the king answered: I would not wish a man more here than I haue . . . But let no man ascribe victorie to our owne strength and might, but onelie to Gods assistance, to whome I haue no doubt we shall worthilie haue cause to giue thanks therefore. And if so be that for our offenses sakes we shall be deliuered into the hands of our enimies, the lesse number we be, the lesse damage shall the realme of England susteine.

28–9 **But if . . . alive** Compare with this speech Hotspur and Falstaff on honor (1 *Henry IV*, I.3.201–8, V.1.131–43, and V.3.61–4).

40 **Crispian** Crispinus and Crispianus, patron saints of shoemakers, were martyred 287 A.D. Their day and that of the battle of Agincourt fell on October 25.

44 **live** Most editors, following Pope, transpose *see* and *live*. Greg and others suggest 'live t' old.'

Act IV, Scene 4

1SD **Excursions** In Q the order of IV.4 and IV.5 is reversed. Compare Pistol's capturing the Frenchman in this scene and the showing up of Pistol in V.1 with Falstaff's claiming the victory over Hotspur (1 *Henry IV*, V.4) or his capturing Colevile (2 *Henry IV*, IV.3) and the attempts to show up Falstaff (1 *Henry*

IV, II.4 and III.3 and so on). Shakespeare patterned Part 2 of *Henry IV* very closely after Part 1, and he repeated some of the patterns of both in this play.

4 Qualtitie . . . me Thus the F. Possibly 'Calen o custure me' (Malone) or 'Callino, castore me' (Boswell). Probably the Irish refrain to a popular Elizabethan song, recited by Pistol to mock the Frenchman.

7–11 O . . . ransom F prints these lines and the following speeches of Pistol as prose: ll. 13–15, 18–20, 22–4, 37–9, 48–9, 65–6.

35–6 à cette heure The spelling in F (*asture*) was a frequent English form of the French phrase. (See III.7.13–14 N.)

37 Owy . . . permafoy See 'Couple a gorge!' at II.1.73.

71–3 roaring . . . dagger Pistol is like the bragging but cowardly Devil of the old morality plays, whose nails the Vice or clown insultingly offered to pare with a wooden dagger.

Act IV, Scene 5

12 die in honor. Once F reads 'dye in once'; Q 'Lets dye with honour.' *Honor* is the word most frequently adopted (after Q) to supply F's missing word. Wilson suggests the more idiomatic 'in harness'; Mason and Walter read 'in arms.'

Act IV, Scene 6

37 kill his prisoners The sudden attack of the French and Henry's orders are historical, and Henry's severity has been variously defended in the light of military codes of the day. Note the reasons for this order given in the following scene, ll. 1–11 and 56–66. Holinshed writes that

> certeine Frenchmen on horssebacke . . . to the number of six hundred horssemen, which were the first that fled, hearing that the English tents & pauilions were a good waie distant from the armie, without anie sufficient gard to defend the same . . . entred vpon the kings campe and there spoiled the hails, robbed the tents, brake vp chests, and caried away caskets and slue such seruants as they found to make anie resistance. . . . But when the outcrie of the lackies and boies which ran away for feare of the Frenchmen thus spoil-

ing the campe, came to the kings eares, he doubting least his enimies should gather togither againe, and begin a new field; and mistrusting further that the prisoners would be an aid to his enimies . . . contrarie to his accustomed gentlenes, commanded by sound of trumpet that euerie man (vpon paine of death) should incontinentlie slaie his prisoner.

Act IV, Scene 7

55SD Bourbon This appears in F. He does not speak (but neither do several of those who enter at V.2 and elsewhere), and most editors omit his name.

56–66 I was . . . them so This appears in Holinshed but not in Hall:

Some write, that the king perceiuing his enimies in one part to assemble togither, as though they meant to giue a new battell for preseruation of the prisoners, sent to them an herald, commanding them either to depart out of his sight, or else to come forward at once, and give battell: promising herewith, that if they did offer to fight againe, not onelie those prisoners which his people alreadie had taken; but also so manie of them as in this new conflict, which they thus attempted should fall into his hands, should die the death without redemption.

67–91 Here comes . . . Agincourt Shakespeare is here very close to Holinshed:

In the morning, Montioie king at armes and foure other French heralds came to the K. to know the number of prisoners, and to desire buriall for the dead. Before he made them answer (to vnderstand what they would saie) he demanded of them whie they made to him that request, considering that he knew not whether the victorie was his or theirs? When Montioie by true and iust confession had cleered that doubt to the high praise of the king, he desired of Montioie to vnderstand the name of the castell neere adioining: when they had told him that it was called Agincourt, he said, Then shall this conflict be called the battell of Agincourt.

100–02 Welshmen . . . caps Nothing else is known of this incident nor of the Welsh custom of wearing leeks in these round, brimless, high-crowned caps. The custom is supposed to commemorate a victory of the Welsh over the Saxons on St. David's Day, March 1, 540. David (*Tavy*) is the patron saint of Wales.

109 **Welsh plood** Henry's great-grandmother was a Welsh princess. Queen Elizabeth herself was descended from Owen Tudor, a Welshman who married Queen Katharine, Henry's widow.

119–20 **Bring . . . parts** The king's request is not satisfied until sc. 8, l. 71, when a herald returns with the information. Since the intervening 135 lines complete the episode of the glove, which may have been added later, it is possible that this scene also underwent revision. Fluellen's apparent failure to recognize Williams at sc. 8, l. 10, after he had confronted him at ll. 133 ff., and the king's sending twice for Gower (at l. 153 and l. 170— thus, however, enabling Fluellen and Williams to meet) may indicate alterations.

162 **doo's** This form (perhaps suggesting pronunciation) is not peculiar to Fluellen's speech, for the king (also Welsh) uses it at III.6.145 and V.2.196 and 227.

Act IV, Scene 8

105 **But . . . twenty** Historically the differences between the French and English losses were apparently staggering. Through their failure to adapt their techniques of conducting mass charges in full armor to the English defensive lines of protected archers, the French, according to Hall and Holinshed, lost 10,000 men (though the latest estimate is 7,000), against a recently estimated English loss of from 400 to 500.

Act V, Prologue

3 **excuse** Between Agincourt and the Treaty of Troyes (1420) five years have elapsed, during which Henry has conducted a second campaign in France.

17–22 **Where . . . God** This appears as follows in Holinshed: 'The king like a graue and sober personage, and as one remembring from whom all victories are sent, seemed little to regard such vaiue [sic] pompe and shewes as were in triumphant sort

155

deuised for his welcomming home from so prosperous a iournie, in so much that he would not suffer his helmet to be caried with him, whereby might haue appeared to the people the blowes and dints that were to be seene in the same.'

30 general The Earl of Essex left London on March 27, 1599, and returned, his attempt to suppress Tyrone's rebellion a failure, on the following September 28. (See Appendix A.)

38 emperor's coming In May 1416 the Holy Roman Emperor, Sigismund, came to England to negotiate between the French king and Henry.

Act V, Scene 1

83–92 Doth . . . wars Pistol refers to Nell Quickly (see II.1.32) as *Doll* here (in both F and Q), and much in this speech may suggest Falstaff. A 'doll' was, however, a woman of easy virtue. (See Appendix A.)

90 steal Pronounced 'stale,' with probable puns on 'urinate' and 'prostitute.' See III.2.44.

Act V, Scene 2

17 balls . . . basilisks A double pun: *balls* refers to both eye-balls and cannon balls, and *basilisks* to large cannon and fabulous serpents, whose glance means death.

36 best garden Compare the following portrait of a disordered garden with two others in *Richard II*—Gaunt's picture of England, the 'other Eden' (II.1), and the Gardener's exact parallel between the commonwealth and nature (III.4).

139 vawting Many of the words in the following passages have double meanings—e.g. *uncoined constancy, tongue, rhyme, reason, wear,* and later *conjure up, circle, hard,* and so on.

350 Praeclarissimus Shakespeare copied a misprint in Holinshed. The French *très-cher* should be paralleled by *praecarissimus,* 'very dear.' Holinshed places this meeting between the French and the English in St. Peter's Church, 'where was a verie ioious meeting betwixt them (and this was on the twentith daie of Maie) and there the king of England, and the ladie Katharine were affianced. After this, the two kings and their councell assembled togither diuerse daies, wherein the first concluded agreement was in diuerse points altered and brought to a certeintie.'

156

APPENDIX A

Text and Date

Problems of text and date relating to *Henry V* are, when compared with the complexity of these matters for many of the plays, relatively simple. Shakespeare rarely refers to clearly datable historical events within his lifetime, but this play contains the only such reference which establishes at once the dates after which and before which the play was probably written. Lines 29–34 in the Prologue to Act V compare the glorious return from France of England's 'conqu'ring Caesar,' King Henry, with that of 'the general of our gracious empress' from Ireland, 'Bringing rebellion broached on his sword.' This general has long been identified with Essex, who left England to establish firmly England's supremacy over Ireland in March 1599 and returned in disgrace the following September. Since public expectation concerning this venture began to wane by June of that year, Shakespeare's high-spirited parallel must have been penned by midsummer. A little earlier the now famous list of plays given by Meres in his *Palladis Tamia* (September 1598) mentions *Henry IV* but not *Henry V*.

We know that *Henry V* was acted by the Chamberlain's men (Shakespeare's company) in 1599. It was printed in 1600 in the small quarto form in which single plays were published, and in two later quartos, derived from the first, in 1602 and again in 1619 (marked 1608). The first of these (Q) is probably a radical abridgment of an acting version of the play, possibly memorized or 'reported' by a pirate actor or actors and sold to a printer for ready money. It is one of the 'Bad' Quartos, shorter than the Folio text by some 1700 lines, and it omits all of the choruses and the Epilogue, three entire scenes (I.1, III.1, and IV.2), and eleven other passages of from about twenty to eighty lines. Except in a few speeches it is so garbled (setting many passages of prose as absurdly irregular verse) that it is useful only in corroborating readings of the Folio or in supplying an occasional word or phrase where the Folio reading is doubtful.

The First Folio (F) of 1623 offers us the only good text of this play. It is probably taken from a manuscript in Shakespeare's hand (his 'foul' papers), from a scribal copy of such a manuscript, or possibly from both. Though several of its proper names are confused (Henry is once called 'Ireland'), though Pistol's speeches are printed as prose, and the French is often almost unintelligible, F affords us a commendable and interesting copy text, in a form (with or without revisions by the author) very similar to that which Shakespeare probably handed his players. Scene divisions are not indicated, and although act divisions are marked carelessly, the position of the five choruses relieves us of all doubt concerning this matter. Lineation is often clearly wrong (most of Pistol's speeches) and sometimes doubtful, but punctuation is as thorough as it is for any of the other plays in F. Pointing is, nevertheless, by modern standards, frequently erratic and excessive, and in this text, except in several passages of colorful prose, it is considerably simplified. By and large (though with many exceptions) the numerous colons in F are here given as periods and the semicolons as commas; many commas are dropped entirely.

The presence in this play of the dialect forms of Fluellen and the other captains (most of which are retained) and of a puzzling version of 16th-century French (here normalized) renders problems of orthography in *Henry V* especially interesting. The glosses call attention to the pronunciation of many words, and many spellings which indicate pronunciation different from our own have been retained, e.g. *Callice* for Calais, *Harflew* for Harfleur, *Dolphin* for Dauphin, *bankrout* for bankrupt, *creeple* for cripple, *perfit* for perfect, *shrowdly* for shrewdly, *venter* for venture, *divel* (also *devil*), *doo'st, farwell, huswife, mervailous, murther, vawting, wrack,* and all significant forms in the dialects of the four captains. The F spellings of other words (like *vp-peer'd*) are indicated in the notes or glosses when important for the meaning or meter of a particular passage. Among the forms not usually noted are *I* for ay, *Ile* for I'll, *wee'l* for we'll, *ore* for o'er, *onely* for only, *shew* for show, and archaic spellings like *howre, yeeres, Iland, Soueraign,* and *Souldiers.* Spellings that for the Elizabethans were completely interchangeable are also not usually indicated: *an, and; loose, lose; than, then,* and *to, too.* Many other interesting spellings (often phonetic) have not ordinarily been retained or glossed: *atchieve, basterd, batcheler, begger, fierie* and *Squier, Gloster, Humfrey, Lyms* (limbs), *perswaded, Reyne* (reign), *shoo* (shoe), *Syens* (scions), and *Marshall* for martial and *Rights* for rites. Problems connected with the French of F are discussed briefly in the notes to III.4, and the original French of this scene is reproduced at the end of this Appendix.

In recent years several irregularities in the F text of *Henry V* have been considered as composite evidence for Shakespeare's working over parts of the original text of the play at a later date, with some specific purpose in mind. The most interesting of the explanations put forth for revision revolves about the possible presence of Falstaff in the first version of the play. Proponents of this theory maintain that Shakespeare then cut the fat knight out for one of several reasons and substituted for him several new scenes or parts of scenes. The passages in question involve II.1 and 3, III.2, and several lines in III.6, in IV.1 and 7–8, and in V.1. Some of the evidence for alteration within these scenes is given in the notes. The Prologue of Act II, for example, prepares us for King Henry's unmasking of the traitors in Southampton and then for scenes in France. But the last two lines of the Prologue seem introduced, rather awkwardly, to account for scenes 1 and 3, which are laid instead in London. These scenes present the merry interchanges of Nym, Bardolph, and Pistol, and culminate in Mistress Quickly's famous description of Falstaff's death. In III.2, furthermore, the Boy's soliloquy (ll. 30–56) and the curiously independent episode of the four captains (ll. 57 ff.) show possible signs of having been altered or added to the original text. Similarly, in IV.1 the speeches of Pistol (as everywhere in the play), the discussion between Henry and the three soldiers about war, the episode of Williams' glove, Henry's famous first soliloquy before Agincourt (ll. 234–88); in IV.7 and 8 the continuation of the glove episode; and in V.1 the capping of the quarrel between Pistol and Fluellen—all may have been altered by Shakespeare.

It is possible that the promise in the Epilogue to 2 *Henry IV* to 'continue the story with Sir John [Falstaff] in it' was originally fulfilled. Then, because of the permanent absence from the Chamberlain's men of the actor who played the part of Falstaff (Will

Kemp), or, more probably, because the Master of the Revels deleted the role out of deference to Lord Cobham (who saw in the part an insult to his family name), or for some other reason, Falstaff was dropped and new material added to the play. In the version handed down to us Pistol may have taken over much of the role of Falstaff, and Shakespeare may have expanded the part of Fluellen and the subplot generally to make up for the loss of his overwhelmingly popular character. In the present form the play is very long—nearly 3,400 lines.

Despite the evidence for major revision in the F text summarized briefly here and in the notes, however, the nature and extent of such revision, and the reasons for it, are still far from clear. Theories about the possible presence of Falstaff in an earlier version of the play raise serious problems about the nature of *Henry V* and its immediate predecessor in the series. After the dramatic rightness of the rejection of Falstaff at the end of 2 *Henry IV*, it is difficult to imagine his being revived to play a role very different from that assigned the buffoon Sir John in *The Merry Wives*. Certainly the presence of the old Falstaff in the world of the reformed and heroic Henry V would greatly alter the nature of this play. If the aging knight once joined the other irregular humorists on the fields of France, clear traces of his presence, in the kinds of recurring themes and images which relate him so profoundly to the two parts of *Henry IV*, have disappeared.

The editor of this edition of *Henry V* is deeply indebted to the careful scholarship of many students of the play. The arguments for revision given above have been developed by Alfred Pollard, Dover Wilson, and G. I. Duthie, and further supported by the detailed evidence of Allan Wilkinson and (especially) J. H. Walter. Of the editions of the play consulted, those by Dover Wilson (Cambridge), G. B. Harrison (Harcourt, Brace), G. L. Kittredge (Ginn), G. C. Moore Smith (Heath), and J. H. Walter (Methuen) have proved to be most helpful. The general editors of the Yale Shakespeare have offered many valuable suggestions.

Act III, Scene 4, in the French of the First Folio

Enter Katherine and an old Gentlewoman.

Kathe. Alice, tu as este en Angleterre, & tu bien parlas le Language.

Alice. En peu Madame.

Kath. Ie te prie m'ensigniez, il faut que ie apprend a parlen: Comient appelle vous le main en Anglois?

Alice. Le main il & appelle de Hand.

Kath. De Hand.

Alice. E le doyts.

Kat. Le doyts, ma foy Ie oublie, e doyt mays, ie me souemeray le doyts ie pense qu'ils ont appelle de fingres, ou de fingres.

Alice. Le main de Hand, le doyts le Fingres, ie pense que ie suis le bon escholier.

Kath. I'ay gaynie diux mots d'Anglois vistement, coment appelle vous le ongles?

Alice. Le ongles, les appellons de Nayles.

Kath. De Nayles escoute: dites moy, si ie parle bien: de Hand, de Fingres, e de Nayles.

Alice. C'est bien dict Madame, il & fort bon Anglois.

Kath. Dites moy l'Anglois pour le bras.

Alice. De Arme, Madame.

Kath. E de coudee.

Alice. D'Elbow.

Kath. D'Elbow: Ie men fay le repiticio de touts les mots que vous maves, apprins des a present.

Alice. Il & trop difficile Madame, comme Ie pense.

Kath. Excuse moy Alice escoute, d'Hand, de Fingre, de Nayles, d'Arma, de Bilbow.

Alice. D'Elbow, Madame.

Kath. O Seigneur Dieu, ie men oublie d'Elbow, coment appelle vous le col.

Alice. De Nick, Madame.

Kath. De Nick, e le menton.

Alice. De Chin.

Kath. De Sin: le col de Nick, le menton de Sın.

Alice. Ouy. Sauf vostre honneur en verite vous pronouncies les mots ausi droict, que le Natifs d'Angleterre.

Kath. Ie ne doute point d'apprendre par de grace de Dieu, & en peu de temps.

Alice. N'aue vos y desia oublie ce que ie vous a ensignie.

Kath. Nome ie recitera a vous promptement, d'Hand, de Fingre, de Maylees.

Alice. De Nayles, Madame.

Kath. De Nayles, de Arme, de Ilbow.

Alice. Sans vostre honeus d'Elbow.

Kath. Ainsi de ie d'Elbow, de Nick, & de Sin: coment appelle vous les pied & de roba.

Alice. Le Foot Madame, & le Count.

Kath. Le Foot, & le Count: O Seignieur Dieu, il sont le mots de son mauvais corruptible grosse & impudique, & non pour le Dames de Honeur d'vser: Ie ne voudray pronouncer ce mots deuant le Seigneurs de France, pour toute le monde, fo le Foot & le Count neant moys, Ie recitera vn autrefoys ma lecon ensembe, d'Hand, de Fingre, de Nayles, d'Arme, d'Elbow, de Nick, de Sin, de Foot, le Count.

Alice. Excellent, Madame.

Kath. C'est asses pour vne foyes, alons nous a diner.

Exit.

APPENDIX B

Sources

Henry V is the ninth and last (if we do not include *Henry VIII*) of the unified series of plays in which Shakespeare dramatizes a memorable succession of events in English history, primarily (*King John* excepted) of the late 14th and the 15th centuries. For it, as for the earlier plays, Shakespeare turned chiefly to the second edition (1587) of Raphael Holinshed's *Chronicles of England, Scotland, and Ireland*. He seems to follow his source more closely for this play than for any of the others—in some places, as in the prolonged airing of Henry's claims to the French throne in I.2, or the listing of the dead after Agincourt in IV.8, versifying Holinshed, phrase by phrase, for many lines at a time. Many of the major scenes of the play—the conspiracy at Southampton, the siege of Harfleur, interchanges at the French court, speeches of Henry to the French herald and to his soldiers, and others—are very close in particular passages to Holinshed's narrative. The selections from the *Chronicles* given in the notes of this edition, however, cannot suggest the unrelaxing alertness of Shakespeare in selecting and organizing details from his source, and the student is urged to consult the full narrative of Henry's reign for himself. Two-thirds of Holinshed's account is concerned with events following Agincourt, but the Prologue to Act V of *Henry V* leaps from 1415 to 1420, across later campaigns in France, to the negotiations at Troyes, where Shakespeare makes us 'merry with fair Katharine of France,' as the Epilogue of *2 Henry IV* had promised. Nearly all of the central and varied scene before Agincourt (IV.1) is Shakespeare's invention, and so, of course, are Pistol and his crew (inherited—all but Nym— from *Henry IV*), the four captains fighting under Henry, and, throughout, the dramatic heightening and structuring that have shaped from the stuff of history a work of art.

Holinshed's account is largely based upon Edward Hall's *The Union of the Two Noble and Illustre Families of Lancaster and York*, 1548. Since Holinshed reproduces many entire passages from Hall with scarcely the change of a word, it is frequently impossible to know when Shakespeare is reading directly from the earlier chronicle. But the passage in which the nobles persuade Henry to go to war (I.2), that in which the Constable describes the English soldiers (IV.2), and several other single words, phrases, or lines seem clearly derived from Hall. More important for Shakespeare than these details, however, was Hall's conception of history, which is far more unified and imaginative than that of Holinshed. Hall's viewing of the course of history from the deposition of Richard II through the victories of Henry V, and beyond, as a single movement, involving divine vengeance and human retribution on a grand scale, doubtless aided Shakespeare greatly in his organizing of the diverse materials that lie behind this related series of plays.

At least three incidents in *Henry V*—the gift of the tennis balls, Pistol's capture of the French soldier, and Henry's wooing of Katharine—are possibly indebted to an old play on the life of Henry, surviving in a corrupted form as *The Famous Victories of Henry the Fift*, registered in 1594. A selection from the wooing scene of this play is given below. It is quite possible that Shakespeare consulted a biography of Henry (the *Gesta Henrici Quinti*) written by a chaplain who accompanied him on his first campaign, and another biography with almost the same title written (by the 'Pseudo-Elmham') about thirty years after his death. Shakespeare's possible further indebtedness to the *Brut*, to the Italian chronicler Tito Livio, the French Le Fèvre or Monstrelet, or the English Fabyan is difficult to prove.

A Portion of the Wooing Scene from 'The Famous Victories of Henry the Fift.'

Katheren. And it please your Maiestie,
  My father sent me to know if you will debate any of these
  Vnreasonable demands which you require:
Hen. 5. Now trust me Kate,
  I commend thy fathers wit greatly in this,
  For none in the world could sooner haue made me debate it
  If it were possible:
  But tell me sweete Kate, canst thou tell me how to loue?
Kate. I cannot hate my good Lord,
  Therefore far vnfit were it for me to loue.

164

Hen. 5. Tush Kate, but tell me in plaine termes,
　Canst thou loue the King of England?
　I cannot do as these Countries do,
　That spend halfe their time in woing:
　Tush wench, I am none such,
　But wilt thou go ouer to England?
Kate. I would to God, that I had your Maiestie,
　As fast in loue, as you haue my father in warres,
　I would not vouchsafe so much as one looke,
　Untill you had related all these vnreasonable demands.
Hen. 5. Tush Kate, I know thou wouldst not vse me so
　Hardly: But tell me, canst thou loue the king of England?
Kate. How should I loue him, that hath dealt so hardly
　With my father.
Hen. 5. But ile deale as easily with thee,
　As thy heart can imagine, or tongue can require,
　How saist thou, what will it be?
Kate. If I were of my owne direction,
　I could giue you answere;
　But seeing I stand at my fathers direction,
　I must first know his will.
Hen. 5. But shal I have thy good wil in the mean season?
Kate. Whereas I can put your grace in no assurance,
　I would be loth to put in any dispaire.
Hen. 5. Now before God, it is a sweete wench.
　　　　　　　　She goes aside, and speaks as followeth.
Kat. I may thinke my selfe the happiest in the world,
　That is beloued of the mightie King of England.
Hen. 5. Well Kate, are you at hoast with me?
　Sweete Kate, tel thy father from me,
　That none in the world could sooner haue perswaded me to
　It then thou, and so tel thy father from me.
Kat. God keepe your Maiestie in good health.
　　　　　　　　　　　　　　　　Exit KAT.

Hen. 5. Farwel sweet Kate, in faith, it is a sweet wench,
　But if I knew I could not haue her fathers good wil,
　I would so rowse the Towers ouer his eares,
　That I would make him be glad to bring her me,
　Upon his hands and knees.
　　　　　　　　　　　　　　　　Exit KING.

APPENDIX C

Reading List

L. B. CAMPBELL, 'The Victorious Acts of King Henry V,' *Shakespeare's 'Histories,'* San Marino, Huntington Library, 1947.

H. GRANVILLE-BARKER, 'From *Henry V* to *Hamlet,'* *Aspects of Shakespeare*, British Academy Lectures, London, Oxford University Press, 1933.

J. PALMER, 'Henry of Monmouth,' *Political Characters of Shakespeare*, London, Macmillan, 1945.

D. J. SNIDER, 'Henry the Fifth,' *Shakespearean Drama: The Histories*, St. Louis, W. H. Miner, 1922.

E. E. STOLL, *Poets and Playwrights*, Minneapolis, University of Minnesota Press, 1930, pp. 31–54.

E. M. W. TILLYARD, *'Henry V,'* *Shakespeare's History Plays*, New York, Macmillan, 1946.

D. A. TRAVERSI, *'Henry the Fifth,'* *The Importance of Scrutiny*, ed. E. Bentley, New York, Stewart, 1948, pp. 120–40.

C. WILLIAMS, *'Henry V,'* *Shakespeare Criticism: 1919–1935*, ed. A. Bradby, London, Oxford University Press, 1936, pp. 180–8.